"Marsha Friedman has given the entrepreneur an edge to understand publicity. How the public perceives you is paramount when it comes to success. I highly recommend this book for everyone who wants to succeed."

—Earl L. Mindell, RPh, MH, PhD

author of sixty-three health-oriented books, including international best-selling *The New Vitamin Bible*, with sales of over 11 million copies

"Nobody does it better! *Gaining the Publicity Edge: An Entrepreneur's Guide to Growing Your Brand Through National Media Coverage* by Marsha Friedman is a down-to-earth guide and model for success in business.

Gaining the Publicity Edge provides entrepreneurs with a step-by-step guide to publicizing their business or cause. But that is not all. As an entrepreneur herself, Friedman takes the reader behind the scenes, encouraging them to look beyond their own wants in promoting their business to the expectations of the media. The media does not exist to promote their business, product, or cause, but to satisfy their audience. Therefore, she encourages entrepreneurs to think outside the box and consider what they can provide to those audiences.

What makes this marketing book unique, along with Friedman's vast expertise in the field of publicity, is the author's voice, which is warm and relatable, making for an easy and enjoyable read. A must read for entrepreneurs who strive for excellence and will settle for nothing less than exceptional."

—Darlene Quinn

author of *Webs of Perception*, the sixth book in her award-winning Web series

"An amazing media work of art! Congratulations to Marsha for taking the complex business discipline of media and compressing it into a working toolkit that brings clarity to what media experts complicate and keep mystical. As an entrepreneur and business owner in a very competitive financial services industry, I have to rely on credible media to pitch my brand, which was not successful in the past because I didn't understand the media concepts and strategies Marsha so eloquently maps out in *Gaining The Publicity Edge*. What Marsha presents in this work of art is a practical playbook on how to win and grow your business in any industry through a national media presence and executing the strategy in the right way by understanding the culture of media. I have been successful working with Marsha on the media tactics she presents and have seen a direct correlation to my business growth and the national media coverage her firm has been able to acquire for my business using the strategies she presents. A must-read for every business owner who wants to stay relevant in their industry, compete at a national level, and simply GROW!"

—Jeannette Bajalia

author of *Retirement Done Right* and *Wi$e Up Women*
president of Petros Estate & Retirement Planning
founder and president of Woman's Worth®,
specializing in women's retirement needs

"If you want to increase your visibility, expand your marketplace credibility, and establish your expertise then you need this book! I have worked with Marsha Friedman and her amazing team for years and the results have been incredible! There is no one today who understands the publicity game like Marsha. And I don't say that lightly. I have worked with many others who profess to be good and the results weren't great. Marsha knows what she's talking about and proves it every time with amazing results! I can't recommend her enough and *Gaining The Publicity Edge* will give you a powerful view of what I am talking about."
—Douglas Vermeeren
international motivational speaker and best-selling author of *Personal Power Mastery*

"As with any difficult thing, a real master makes it look easy, and reading Marsha Friedman's book is like being mentored by the consummate master in her field of publicity. Her advice gives you the needed edge to cut through the noise to get your message through. It is pure wisdom. After only a few pages, you'll realize why she is the best at gaining the edge for her clients. Bravo, Marsha!"
—Paul Friederichsen
brand marketing consultant

"Today's world is filled with a sea of noise on TV, on radio, and in print, and trying to break through to get publicity for your brand can be a daunting challenge. But in her book, *Gaining the Publicity Edge*, Marsha Friedman explains how to rise above the clamor, grab the media's attention, and leverage the results to gain the edge over your competition. Her book is a must read for anyone who wants to build their brand and be recognized as a leading authority in their field."

—Gary Miliefsky

cyber security expert and publisher of *Cyber Defense Magazine*

"This book is a must-read for any entrepreneur or marketing executive focused on business growth and brand awareness. It doesn't matter if you are just getting started with a shoestring marketing budget or if you're the chief marketing officer at a Fortune 500 company; the PR game has changed. You need to understand how it works to win. Marsha is a genius at crafting pitches that work in our fast-paced, Internet-obsessed world, and she shares detailed secrets that get the attention and media coverage you need. There is more competition than ever in today's business world and media coverage gives you credibility your competitors don't have. It makes you stand out as a leader in your industry. Marsha's pitches have landed my name in *Forbes, The New York Daily News*, national radio shows, and more. Reading and implementing this book will make a massive impact on your business and the longevity of your personal brand."

—Lauren Davenport

CEO, The Symphony Agency

GAINING THE
PUBLICITY EDGE

GAINING THE PUBLICITY EDGE

AN ENTREPRENEUR'S GUIDE
TO GROWING YOUR BRAND
through national media coverage

MARSHA FRIEDMAN

ForbesBooks

Published by ForbesBooks, Charleston, South Carolina.
Member of Advantage Media Group.

ForbesBooks is a registered trademark, and the ForbesBooks colophon is a trademark of Forbes Media, LLC.

Printed in the United States of America.

10 9 8 7 6 5 4 3 2 1

ISBN: 978-1-946633-91-0
LCCN: 2019937169

Book design by Melanie Cloth.

This publication is designed to provide accurate and authoritative information in regard to the subject matter covered. It is sold with the understanding that the publisher is not engaged in rendering legal, accounting, or other professional services. If legal advice or other expert assistance is required, the services of a competent professional person should be sought.

Advantage Media Group is proud to be a part of the Tree Neutral® program. Tree Neutral offsets the number of trees consumed in the production and printing of this book by taking proactive steps such as planting trees in direct proportion to the number of trees used to print books. To learn more about Tree Neutral, please visit www.treeneutral.com.

Since 1917, the Forbes mission has remained constant. Global Champions of Entrepreneurial Capitalism. ForbesBooks exists to further that aim by bringing the Stories, Passion, and Knowledge of top thought leaders to the forefront. ForbesBooks brings you The Best in Business. To be considered for publication, please visit www.forbesbooks.com.

To my husband, Steve, and my children, Damon, Elon, and Ari.
Your love and devotion is my greatest treasure;
each of you will always be such a blessing in my life …

To my daughter, Adina, who has passed; you will always hold
a special place in my heart …

VISIT US ONLINE TO ACCESS THESE FREE RESOURCES

How do your press hits rank against your competitors?

When the media needs a reliable source to interview for their publication or on their show, they look to a select few experts to answer the call. Do you qualify to be one of their go-to authorities?

→ **Take the assessment at newsandexperts.com/assessment to find out.**
   Your score will be emailed to you within seconds of submitting.

Subscribe to our newsletter.

Sign up for the PR Insider Newsletter to receive weekly publicity tips to get you featured in the press and on radio and TV.

→ **Subscribe at newsandexperts.com/newsletter.**

Get In Touch

Our team is always ready to assist you with all your Public Relations needs and we look forward to your questions and comments.

→ **Reach out by emailing info@newsandexperts.com or calling 800.204.7115.**

CONTENTS

FOREWORD

There is a difference in being different and making a difference. Marsha Friedman makes a difference in people's lives, pure and simple.

Almost thirty years ago, Marsha turned the PR world upside down when she started her own firm in Tampa, Florida. For the first time, a public relations firm actually guaranteed results! Through this totally different business model, Marsha grew her agency into one of the most respected independent PR firms around, attracting scores of clients all wanting to promote their products, books, or expertise all over the country.

As a former vice-chairman for Saatchi & Saatchi Worldwide, I have worked with some of the largest PR firms there are, from Edelman to Hill+Knowlton. But none have had the authentic street smarts and skill sets for publicity like Marsha Friedman. I should know, because I've had the pleasure of working with her on many projects.

Chances are you may never have the same opportunity to work alongside her as I have. But you're in luck. The book you're now holding, *Gaining the Publicity Edge*, is pure Marsha. It's plainspoken, easy to understand, and filled with straight-from-the-shoulder advice from one entrepreneur to another. This could be the best book on the subject I've ever read, and in fact it's probably the only book on publicity you'll ever need.

Amazingly, I've never agreed to write the foreword to a book on marketing, advertising, or public relations until now. When Marsha asked if I would consider doing this, I jumped at the chance. Why? Because I know if you read this book, you'll be the better for having done so. Let Marsha Friedman's wisdom and experience make a difference in your business and your life. Find your publicity edge ... pure and simple.

—Jim Lindsey
vice-chairman (retired)
Saatchi & Saatchi Advertising Worldwide

ACKNOWLEDGMENTS

As I began to think about who to acknowledge for their contributions to this new book, I realized that the acknowledgements needed to go back much further than the book's birth. I can't help but to be grateful to the initial clients who were there at the launch of my PR firm nearly thirty years ago; they believed in me enough to allow me to represent them as I learned to work with the media and gain an understanding of their needs and how to serve them.

So, yes, those first clients deserve a big thank you three decades later for the role they played as I set off on my journey to becoming a successful entrepreneur, an innovator, and an award-winning influencer in my field.

Because this book explains in great detail, but in simple terms, how the media works and how to secure publicity—things not taught in any college classroom or even learned in most PR agencies—I'm also grateful to the thousands of clients we subsequently represented over the course of nearly thirty years of business. These clients provided the hands-on experience with the media and the empirical evidence to support the information I've shared in this book. Even the campaigns that didn't get the coverage we had hoped for proved to be learning experiences as we examined our mistakes and figured out how to correct them.

As you might imagine, I'm also very grateful to the many wonderful team members who passed through our doors since 1990, and who contributed to those learning experiences and the great results we achieved for our clients.

I'm especially grateful to the current team members who continue to navigate the media's changing landscape and secure amazing national press for our clients. Special thanks to Rachel Friedman, who took over managing the company's operations so that I've been able to move beyond the day-to-day functions; Miguel Casellas-Gil, who took on the senior publicity director role and overall management of our clients' campaigns; Jay York, who is my "go-to" authority for anything related to social media and whose guidance on the book's cover design was precious; Freda Drake, our vice president of business development; Dan Dunkin, one of our very talented on-staff writers; Ashley Pontius, Terry Stanton, Dave Purdy and Nick DiMeo, who are all interacting directly with the media every day; Brittany Thomas, the company's energetic "enforcer"; and last but not least, Jen Lee and Jen Harden, the administrative backbone of our team. Also, thanks to Marti Carlson, who was my executive assistant for ten years, and who made sure my every need was taken care of so I could run the company effectively. And a very special thank you to Ronnie Blair, our senior writer who worked closely with me in the editing process so that I was happy with my message.

These acknowledgements wouldn't be complete without expressing my thanks to Adam Witty, founder of Advantage Media Group|Forbes Books. Adam encouraged me to write this book in order to impart my experiences and insights to anyone who is serious about reaching out to the media, sharing their knowledge with others, and building their brand as an authority in their field.

Finally, my deepest appreciation to any and everyone who played a role—large or small—in what has been a marvelous and extraordinary journey.

INTRODUCTION

"People don't believe what you say about yourself, but they sure do believe what other people say about you!"

The above adage is one I've known for years. Fortunately, I learned it early in my entrepreneurial career, and it has served me well. When I started my business many years ago, I worked hard to be a "darling of the media." Truth be told, I still do today. Every time I or my company is featured in the media and receives publicity, the cash register rings or a new door opens. I'm constantly amazed by the third-party credibility and validation the media can provide a business.

I met Marsha Friedman in 2008. As a book publisher for entrepreneurs and business owners, I immediately connected the dots and understood how Marsha's company could help my authors get free publicity.

Marsha and her company have been so successful in getting so much free publicity for my authors. I was left with only one logical choice: I needed to buy her company. Finally, after many years of making me wait, News & Experts joined the Advantage Family in 2018.

I asked Marsha to author a simple book that would teach entrepreneurs how to make themselves and their businesses attractive to the media. *This is that book*. Free publicity and media grows businesses. This book shows you how.

—Adam Witty
Founder and CEO, Advantage Media Group

CHAPTER ONE

THE POWER OF PUBLICITY

I t was a protein bar, of all things, that reinforced for me the power of publicity.

When my publicity firm was just a few years old, a new client came to us: a Japanese start-up company whose product was a protein bar. The wealthy Japanese gentleman who owned the company flew out to meet with me. He told me he wanted us to book his spokesperson as a guest on talk radio shows around the country, because that was the best medium to promote a brand—which, in the 1990s, was absolutely true.

"We can certainly do that," I said. "But, as we charge a flat fee for each radio interview, what's your budget for this campaign?"

"There's no limit," he replied. "I want you to book as many interviews as you possibly can."

"How many do you think that is?" I asked.

"Twenty a month," I said, mentally crossing my fingers.

"Can you book thirty?" he asked.

I did a quick calculation in my head. If he wanted to pay for thirty interviews a month, how could I say no? We were a young company, and I knew I needed to make it happen. "Yes!" I said. "We'll figure it out!"

Fortunately, I knew enough about what would make a good talk radio interview, plus the company had a great spokesperson with whom we'd worked before. He could talk about anything health related and also knew how to tie it back to the company's product. We all had a vested interest in making it work—we wanted our young company to be a success, after all—so we made it happen. Interview after interview, week in and week out, the spokesperson gave thirty interviews a month for a year.

We were all quite proud of ourselves for pulling it off. Then, at the end of the year, the company ended the contract without giving us any reason.

Naturally, I was disheartened, thinking the campaign had been a failure. Why else would the company cancel the contract? We moved on and continued our work. The experience, though painful, faded into the background as we found success with many other clients. We never heard from the company, and I figured they had gone out of business.

Then, out of the blue, I got a phone call from the protein bar company's spokesperson. It turned out that my assumption that the campaign and the company had failed couldn't have been more wrong. When the company came to me, the spokesperson told me, they were at about $6 million in revenue. A year later, they ended our contract—because their revenue had grown to $60 million. He told me that thanks to the talk radio campaign, they had become so successful they no longer felt the need for our services.

Although clearly I already believed in the power of publicity, it was at this moment I truly understood just how phenomenal publicity can be for an individual, a company, and a brand—if it's done correctly.

And that's still true today. For nearly three decades, I've been at the helm of one of the most successful boutique PR firms in the United States, helping thousands of top professionals develop and enjoy the status of being known in the media and in society at large as the leading expert in their field. As the founder and CEO of EMSI Public Relations, now known as News & Experts, I was one of the pioneers in the game-changing pay-for-performance model of PR. Armed with only a background in marketing and an incredible desire and need to succeed, I set out to create a different kind of PR firm, one that would guarantee results. While it hasn't always been an easy road, it worked.

As a businessperson myself, I know how challenging it is to make a company thrive and grow. That's why I am a true believer in the power of publicity, and why I've dedicated my career to educating others. I've mentored, advised, and worked with a long list of corporate executives, entrepreneurs, and business owners in numerous industries, along with a few political luminaries and celebrities. And I wouldn't want to be doing anything else—especially given how exciting the world of publicity is today.

The twenty-four-seven news cycle, emerging internet technologies, and the social media explosion have created completely new frontiers and a huge media monster that must be fed constantly. Businesspeople wanting to harness the power of publicity are in the best position they've ever been in, because every media outlet is clamoring for unique content—including yours.

What Is Publicity?

Let's talk about what publicity actually is. By definition, publicity is not advertising; it is coverage by the media of people, events, and issues deemed to be of interest to their audiences. Publicity sets any business, practice, or firm apart from its competition by providing the credibility and visibility that's lacking in other forms of marketing.

That credibility comes from the implied endorsement of the journalists and talk show hosts who turn to you as an authoritative source of information. When radio and TV personalities demonstrate their trust in you by interviewing you for a show segment, and when print journalists look to you for information or insight, in essence they're saying, "This is a credible, knowledgeable businessperson."

As a result, the audience is more willing to trust you because you've earned the confidence of media professionals. That kind of credibility can't be bought.

In terms of visibility, publicity tells people who you are, where you are, why you're special, and what you have to offer them. Without it, no matter how wonderful your business, product, book, or services, people are unlikely to come looking.

The nice thing about publicity is that you don't have to pay for it. If you can get a journalist or talk show host interested in your story idea or topic, you might be interviewed for an article or invited to be interviewed as a guest on a radio or TV show. The endorsement of traditional media, even if it's simply mentioning your name, is what I like to call "marketing gold" to anyone trying to build a brand, promote a business, or sell a product.

Thanks to the internet, the value of that gold is through the roof. The internet has opened up so many new opportunities for marketing, but at the same time, it vastly expands the number of competitors in any given field. Potential customers have more options than ever, so what makes one business or professional more trustworthy and appealing than another? One answer is the implied endorsements of TV and radio show hosts, traditional newspapers and magazines—and now, bloggers, news websites, and followers on social media.

Publicity helps level the playing field, says one of our long-term clients. "Publicity gives even the smallest companies the credibility they need to compete in the marketplace. It gives you as much clout as the big boys."

A common misconception is that you have to be a major player to get publicity. But I'm here to tell you that you don't have to be the CEO of a large company, a rock star, a celebrity, or an elected official.

The media are always looking for experts who are accessible and can provide insights on topics in the news.

Now, you might be thinking, "Am I really an expert?" The answer is that anyone with strong credentials, real-life experience, and valuable information to share is seen as an expert by the media.

Beyond degrees and a professional career, your life experience can also make you an expert. For example, we had one client who's a survivor of domestic and child abuse, and who wrote a best-selling book that provides a perspective on how to overcome such a background and thrive as a successful adult. Another client built and sold six successful companies, and now focuses on helping other entrepreneurs by sharing his failures and successes. We had yet another client who survived cancer and shared the emotional, spiritual, and health programs that got him through. The list is long, but being perceived as an expert all boils down to people helping people by sharing their knowledge and experience.

Getting Started

In order to bring your message to market, you need commitment, perseverance, and a plan.

In this book, you'll find the keys I've developed over the course of my career to help you achieve the level of publicity you desire. I'll share with you exactly what's needed to become the go-to person in the media, as well as a trusted authority in your field in the eyes of the people who matter most—your customers.

As all of the material in the book reflects the fact that we live in an age driven by social media, I've also included an entire chapter addressing exactly what you need to do in these platforms as well.

In addition, I'm including a chapter on why we are in a uniquely favorable time for women in business to incorporate publicity as a key component of their marketing strategy. Women today are not only sought after as experts by the media, they are also one of the most important audiences to cultivate.

Are you ready to harness the power of publicity? Then let's dive in!

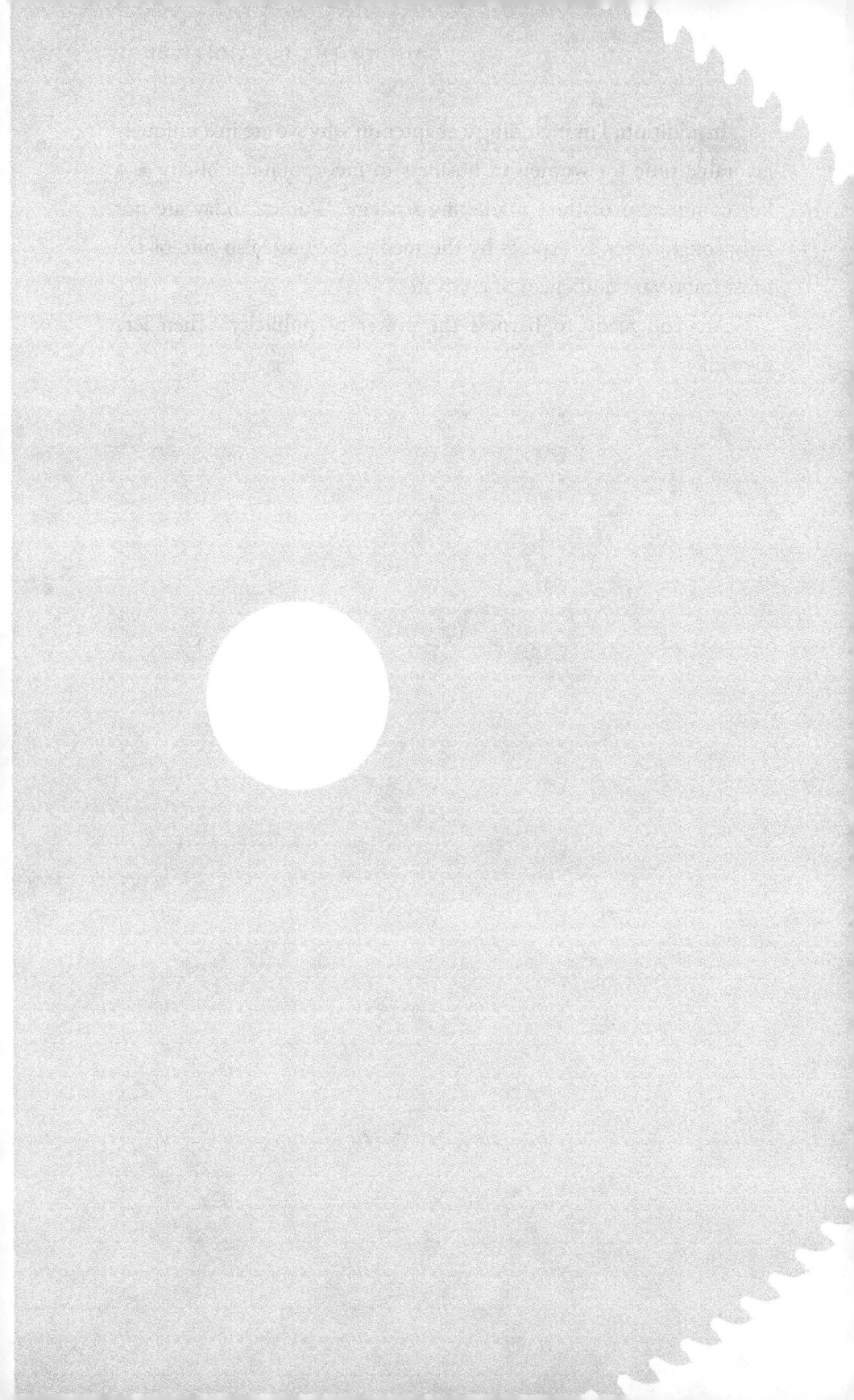

CHAPTER TWO

HOW TO GET ON THE MEDIA'S PLAYING FIELD

If you want to succeed in the publicity game, you need to look at the world from the media's point of view and consider how your message will interest their audience.

Keep in mind that you and the media have similar but different goals. You're determined to promote your personal or company brand, establish yourself as an authority in your field, and then leverage that publicity to solidify and maintain your brand as an expert. The media, on the other hand, want to provide useful or interesting information that will keep their readers, viewers, or listeners tuned in and coming back for more.

If you're going to invest in publicity because you realize its power and value, it's important to understand the media and their business model. Just as you want to build your business, the media want to build theirs. For the media, it's the size of their audience; for you, it may be the size of your customer base. But this is where your goals align.

I learned this lesson early on when I launched my company with the pay-for-performance model of PR.

Unlike other agencies, we only got paid for interviews we secured. To accomplish that, I had to learn how the media operates and what their needs were. It was clear that to be successful, I'd need to serve two clients: those who pay me to get them in the media, and also the media themselves by giving them quality content and experts to interview for their shows and publications. I understood that if my company could serve the media's needs in the same way we serve our clients' needs, we'd have a win-win situation for the media, our clients, and ourselves.

One of the things I learned early on was that the standard press release was dead—despite the fact that it's still taught in colleges and universities around the country to students who want to build a career in public relations. It was a simple lesson to learn when I started out and saw that press releases got little to no response from the media.

I needed my communication to the media to elicit a positive response: "Yes, I would love to schedule your client as a guest on my show!" In those early days, that "yes" response determined if I was going to take home a paycheck that week. So, being a marketer at heart, I threw away the sample press releases I'd read in the library and put on my marketing hat instead. I was intent on figuring out how to get a "yes" from the media to feature my clients on their shows so I could earn a living.

My answer was to go back to basic marketing principles. I asked myself all of the marketing 101 questions: First, who was my target audience? When I first launched my business, I was only booking my clients on talk radio shows; in those days, it was the best medium for getting your message across. So, my target audience was radio show producers and hosts. The second question was: Why would they want to have my client on their show? How would it benefit them and their listeners?

As a listener of talk radio myself, I was a dedicated fan of shows that had guests who covered a variety of topics and enhanced my life with valuable information. If I could show a producer how my clients could engage their audience, I knew I could get a "yes" with a date for the interview. Why? Because if the interview with my client kept listeners tuned in, it would help the show's ratings—which makes the host happy, as ratings are a reflection of the quality of their show, and it'd make the station happy because higher ratings mean higher advertising rates.

With this realization in mind, I started developing interview segments with a bold headline that gave a concept of what the interview would be about, followed by the meat of the topic along with questions for the host to ask. Once I saw how well this worked, I was able to secure more bookings, bring in more money, and grow my company.

It didn't take me long to realize that our success came because we made the media's job easier. We gave hosts and producers everything they needed to do a great interview, without them having to spend valuable time doing their own research about the topic, coming up with questions, and so on.

We worked this out for talk radio, then carried it over to TV and the press, and found that this formula worked for all types of media.

Our pay-for-performance model forced me to understand the inner workings of the media, which allowed my company to develop the best techniques for playing the media game. Now I'm happy to share with you what we've learned.

The Media's Formula

We know how to engage the media's interest in our clients because we understand their formula—and if you know the formula, you'll be able to engage their interest as well. It's simple: the media, to a large degree, work in terms of problems and solutions. In articles and on talk radio and TV shows, they'll address problems that are common to the masses and bring in experts to interview who can provide solutions. This is how they keep their audience tuned in.

Hosts, producers, and editors know who's listening or watching. They know their demographic—they know their audience's lifestyle, their financial and educational status, and their careers. They know the pulse of their audience—what they're thinking about, what issues they're interested in, and what problems they're living with. And they know what kinds of experts to bring on to address those issues and offer solutions to those problems. They want to talk about what is relevant to their audience now—what is directly affecting them today.

Put yourself in the media's shoes and think about their audience the same way they do. What problems can you address for their audience? What solutions can you offer? That's what keeps the audience happy and tuned in—which is the media's goal.

You Don't Choose the Media, They Choose You

When new clients tell me they want to make sure we get them on the "right" show for their message, I chuckle, because the media wouldn't be interested in them if they thought the message wasn't right for their audience.

Here's a good example: One of my clients, a key figure in a presidential administration, had just published his memoir. We were hired by his publishing company to do a big media campaign to promote the book. My team and I got together with him in his Washington, DC, office, where we sat around a big conference table talking about the media. Our client had close personal relationships with people like Barbara Walters, Diane Sawyer, and Connie Chung, and he was a big-name figure, so he thought—as did we—that we could pick and choose the best show to promote his book.

We tested the waters by reaching out to the executive producers of those shows, expecting positive responses from everyone. Instead, we received a call back directly from Barbara Walters, saying how happy she was that our client, her friend, had released his memoir. But unfortunately, her executive producer felt an interview with him wasn't going to be the right fit for her show. Soon after, we got calls from the other shows—not directly from Diane Sawyer and Connie Chung, but from their executive producers—sharing the same message.

Even the close personal relationships our client had with those national celebrity show hosts did not guarantee that they would automatically take the interview. We had to go with Plan B—which, frankly, turned out to be more valuable for him. We wound up getting him a whole segment on *60 Minutes*, which was a better audience for his book and message. But we learned a hard lesson along the way: it doesn't matter what personal relationships you have; it's whether the media believes that you and your message are the right fit for their show. They will only have you on as a guest if they feel your message is going to engage their audience and keep them tuned in. So, make sure your message is the right fit for their audience or they'll pass you by—no matter what personal connection you have.

How the Media Is Monetized

The media's focus is on building their audience—just like you and I want to build our customer and client base. The bigger the audience for radio and TV shows, the higher their ratings and the more they can charge for advertising. Same thing for the press—the larger their circulation, the more they can charge for ad space. Simply put, the media want to keep their readers reading, listeners listening, and viewers viewing.

That's why they always need experts to comment on the news. Endless news cycles always call for fresh and knowledgeable information to keep viewers, readers, and listeners tuned in. Behind your TV screen, out of earshot on your radio, and just past the boldface print of your newspaper and web pages hustles a busy industry of people who, quite literally, "make the news." This nonstop, twenty-four-hour process requires massive amounts of material to keep moving. There is no shortage of opportunity to share your expertise—if you can provide what the media is looking for.

Along with making money from advertising, the media also want to reduce expenses, because their revenue has decreased significantly in recent years. Today, fewer and fewer advertising dollars are being spent on traditional media, as many advertisers have learned that they can advertise more effectively and efficiently online. They have realized that it's far less expensive to advertise on social media and that you can target your audience in a very granular way. On Facebook you can say, "I want to reach people in this particular income bracket, who live in this particular affluent neighborhood, who have kids this age." That's impossible to do with traditional advertising in traditional media outlets.

As a result of lower revenues, some media outlets have gone completely out of business, while others have downsized or moved entirely online. For online publications, there's a huge competition for views, and to compete, publications need plenty of content—which experts like you can provide. Because newspapers are short staffed, they are eager for high-quality content. According to data from the Occupational Employment Statistics survey conducted by the US Bureau of Labor Statistics, 39,210 people worked as reporters, editors, photographers, or film and video editors in the newspaper industry in 2017. That was down 15 percent from 2014 and 45 percent from 2004.[1]

---

1   "Trends and Facts on Newspapers: State of the News Media," Pew Research Center, June 13, 2018, http://www.journalism.org/fact-sheet/newspapers/.

As bad as these statistics sound for the newspaper industry, it creates an opportunity for you. If you provide good quality, well-written content that fits their format and will engage their readers, they'll be inclined to publish it.

All of this is true for TV and radio as well. Although these media operate a little differently than print media, the goal is the same: if you can provide them with an engaging topic for an interview with you that will keep their listeners tuned in, they're much more likely to bring you on as a guest.

Quid Pro Quo

The great news is, serving the media's needs is a win-win situation. If you are a good guest, then the host will promote you as an expert, touting your book, product, service, or website.

One client wrote me a thank-you note specifically about the introduction the talk radio hosts gave him before they brought him on as a guest. He was floored by it, because it made him sound so amazing. But the host doesn't do this just to boost the guest's ego—they want to spotlight your highest credentials and your greatest achievements, because the more important they make you sound, the more important they seem for having you as a guest on their show.

❈ ❈ ❈

Once you understand the media and can meet their needs, you'll be on your way to building your brand through the coverage you deserve as an expert in your field.

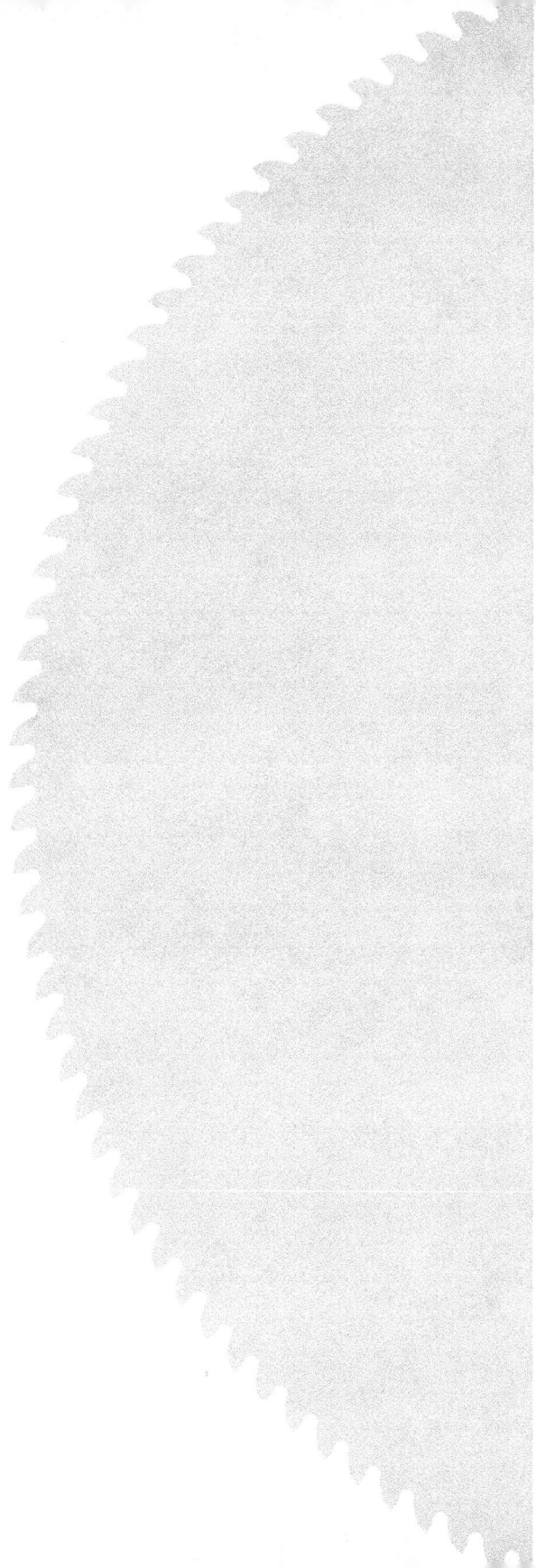

CHAPTER THREE

WHICH MEDIUM IS THE BEST MATCH FOR YOU AND YOUR MESSAGE?

Now that you've decided to get into the media game, there are two key factors to consider. One is to determine which medium has the audience that will be the best fit for your message. The other is to decide which medium you're going to be most comfortable with.

Which Medium Is Right for Your Message?

When figuring out the best type of media for your message, you first need to know who your target audience is.

I had a client, a cardiologist, who'd written a book about diets, recipes, exercise, and vitamin regimens for a healthy heart. The book had a broad market, but this particular theme also included a well-identified niche market: the natural health consumer. So, in addition to going out to the general interest publications, we booked our cardiologist as a guest on a variety of health talk radio shows, whose audiences were more oriented toward natural health. We also pursued coverage for him in publications that appealed to people who shop in health food stores. In his case, crafting his message to media outlets with niche audiences was smart marketing.

Another client, whose military-related book was published by a top university press, admitted that when his publisher asked about his book's audience, he gave the obvious answers—historians, military buffs, sociologists, and so on. But after his book was published, he found that there was a bigger "stealth audience": the wives and mothers whose husbands and sons had been killed in military action, as his book also included how the military deals with soldiers killed in action. That was a very different audience than he originally envisioned, and it gave us a new angle to pitch to media outlets with an audience that included wives and mothers. It also gave this author a brand-new market to cultivate for speaking engagements, book signings, and other promotions.

It's always worthwhile to think outside the box when it comes to your audience. I can guarantee that you have more than one audience that would be interested in your message. In fact, you can sometimes get in front of an audience in a completely unexpected way if you are open to the opportunity.

One client wrote a book on captive insurance, which is a form of insurance that businesses buy into to protect themselves—clearly a pretty obscure topic.

One day, when we got a call for an interview that had nothing to do with his carefully crafted message about captive insurance, we reached out to him. A journalist we work with at *The Wall Street Journal* was doing a story on how different CEOs relieve stress in their lives, and she asked if we had any CEOs who would be interested in being interviewed. We knew this client would be happy to participate even though the topic was unrelated to his message. He understood that being quoted in *The Wall Street Journal* gave a boost to his authority, as he was now included as a "top CEO" in an iconic business publication.

He was excited when friends and associates from all over the country called him up, asking, "Hey, I just read an article in *The Wall Street Journal*—is that you?"

Around the same time, we had another client with a very different take on the media. She had also written a book for a very niche audience, but she was only interested in talking about the very specific issues of her specialty. We couldn't convince her to speak with any mainstream publications that would validate her position as an expert.

We knew these mass-market publications wouldn't be writing articles about the topic of her book. Articles on that subject would more likely appear in industry publications.

We tried to explain to her that while she was an expert in her field, she was also a very successful entrepreneur, a happily married wife, and a mother. She was someone who'd found that elusive balance between professional success and a wonderful family life. It was absolutely something she could talk about with these mainstream publications, which their audiences would be eager to read. Even though she wasn't talking about her niche specialty, it would position her as a top professional in her field.

Often, much to our frustration, clients turn down media interview requests because they don't see the reporter's angle as the right fit. These clients have specific messages they want to push, and though they are qualified to discuss the topic the reporter is calling about, they view doing so as getting "off message," so they pass.

That's a mistake. An article's focus doesn't have to align perfectly with your message for the interview to help build your credibility. In a perfect world, the two would mesh seamlessly, but in the real world, it can be enough that you end up being quoted in major press. That media appearance serves as a third-party endorsement, so once the article appears, you should do as much publication name-dropping as you can. Plus, with a little skill you can often steer the interview toward what you really want to say.

The first step for a good publicity campaign is to get on the playing field. If you aren't in the game, nothing is going to happen. In my experience, the people who have some of the best publicity campaigns are those willing to snatch every opportunity that arises, from the local weekly newspaper to major broadcast operations.

Momentum can't build if you don't get the ball rolling and keep it rolling.

Which Medium Is Right for You?

We all have different personalities. We all have different comfort zones—which not only differ from each other, but constantly change relative to where we are in our lives. When we're at our best, we talk more freely and entertain more easily, our message flows more smoothly, and we're willing to share more and more of ourselves in our effort to inspire and to motivate.

So, if you are new at the publicity game, it's best to start where you feel most comfortable, and where your message will be most readily accepted. Some people would never feel comfortable before a TV camera, but they might enjoy the opportunity to get behind a radio microphone. Others might be more comfortable with the printed word, interviewing for newspapers and magazines.

I believe in doing what works for you. I've counseled enough clients to know that you can't force people to stray too far from their comfort zones. This isn't to suggest that you should only ever target one form of media—radio, TV, print, or social media—and focus your energies solely in that one direction. The world is too multidimensional for that approach. My goal here is simply to help you find the medium that is best for you.

Each medium has its own pros and cons. For instance, one big advantage of talk radio is that there's a show for virtually any topic. Radio requires no travel (all interviews are done by phone from your home or office) and keeps us less exposed than on television.

Still, radio isn't ideal for everyone. Suppose you're an interior designer or a professional photographer, or you want to feature a new line of clothes or jewelry. Radio wouldn't be the best medium, because it's not visual. Television and print would be far better choices, since you can demonstrate your products on TV or use photos to tell your story in print.

Before you begin your media strategy, look at your message and your comfort zone. Once you've done that, let's look at what each of these four types of mediums have to offer.

PRESS

What Makes Being Interviewed by the Press a Great Opportunity?

Print is king! I repeat: print is king! Why? Because anything written is perceived to be valid, so being quoted in the press gives you unquestionable positioning as an authority in your field.

Plus, newspapers, magazines, and blogs are where your customers live. According to a 2016 Nielsen Scarborough study, more than 169 million American adults read daily newspapers, either in print or online.[2] There are publications on topics ranging from antiques to zoology. That is perhaps the most attractive aspect of print media: the huge variety of publications you can target—daily and weekly newspapers, local and national magazines, trade publications, and blogs. The options are endless.

---

2   Paul Fletcher, "Good News for Newspapers: 69% Of U.S. Population Still Reading," *Forbes*, December 26, 2016, https://www.forbes.com/sites/paulfletcher/2016/12/26/ good-news-for-newspapers-69-of-u-s-population-still-reading.

The Advantages of Online Press

Just about everything that appears in print is republished online. That means every article or column that includes a mention of you or your company is likely to appear online, turning up in search engine results and other news aggregators.

Clients used to tell me that they weren't quite as excited about articles that appear online, but today, most people understand their value. The majority of publications today reach significantly more people online than they do with print. For example, *USA Today* has an average daily paid circulation Monday through Friday of 726,906, but online had nearly 97.4 million unique visitors and 1.2 billion page views in April 2018 alone.[3]

That number of eyes coming across an article wouldn't have been possible back in the days when traditional print was the only game in town. Beyond the incredible reach, online print coverage is also easier to share than hard copy. Rather than going out, buying a copy of the paper, cutting out the article and putting it in the mail, you simply email a link. Plus, you can post it on your website and social media so that everyone can see it.

Speaking of your website, online articles can more reliably send readers to your site. Online articles often come with hyperlinks, so if an article includes a link to your website, a reader can click on it right then and immediately learn about you and your brand. If they're reading the article the old-fashioned way, they will have to remember to look you up later, and it may slip their mind.

Online articles are also longer lasting. One concern I hear about online print is that eventually the article will cease to be available online. While it's true that news organizations don't keep articles

---

3   "About *USA Today*," *USA Today*, accessed January 29, 2019, https://marketing.usatoday.com/about.

online forever, the shelf life of traditional print is even shorter. A monthly magazine is off retail shelves in one month. A daily newspaper is usually tossed into a recycling bin within twenty-four hours. The life span of the online version is practically eternal in comparison.

Those online articles can also be helpful if you're trying to get booked as a guest on TV and radio shows. Producers who do a quick search for your name online may find the articles that have featured you as a source, which helps establish your credibility as an expert in your field. These articles are also good fodder for sharing on your social networks. Sharing links to interesting news stories inspires engagement among users—and all the better if those stories feature you, as it boosts your credibility to your followers.

None of this is meant to devalue the traditional versions of newspapers and magazines. Having your name appear in the ink-on-paper version certainly adds to your credibility as a go-to expert in your field, just as it always has. But online takes that a step further and has become the foundation for marketing in the digital age.

What You Need to Know About Press Interviews

One terrific aspect of this medium is that sometimes a journalist offers you the opportunity to provide your comments in writing. While this takes time, it adds the benefit of preparation.

It's different when a journalist is writing a timely story on a tight deadline. They may want to speak with you at a moment's notice. More and more frequently, journalists from big publications like *The New York Times*, *The Wall Street Journal*, and *USA Today* will call us in the morning and say, "I'm on a tight deadline; do you have an expert I can interview for a story I'm doing?" Then, we'll see the story come out that very afternoon, usually by 5:00 p.m.

When such opportunities arise, you need to be ready to respond or else the journalist will move on to find another expert. We had a client who was a big manufacturer of products used in dental labs. The company CEO told me his dream was to be quoted in *The New York Times*.

When we got a call from a *New York Times* reporter who wanted to interview him, we were all high-fiving in the hallway. We immediately called him—but got stonewalled by his secretary. "You don't understand," we said, "*The New York Times* wants to interview your boss! You need to make him available. It can be in a couple of hours, but we need to get him on the line with this journalist!"

"I'm sorry," said the secretary. "I can't interrupt him. He's in an important meeting all day, and I've been given strict orders not to interrupt him. He won't be out until 5:00 p.m."

We tried to get the secretary to listen, or to get around her, but nothing worked. Finally, at 5:00 p.m., our client got out of his meeting—and heard from his secretary that we'd called about an interview with *The New York Times*. He called us immediately, but it was too late.

Our client was devastated. "Please, call the reporter back," he begged. "Please apologize. See if we can reschedule it. I'm available now!" We went through the motions, but we knew it wasn't going to happen. Sure enough, the journalist had moved on to another story and another interview.

If you decide to get into the game of publicity, you have to understand the rules. And one of the rules is that the media works on their time, not yours.

Press Interviews: The Basics

- Phone interviews with journalists vary in length, but can average ten to fifteen minutes, providing enough time for journalists to ask their questions and take notes of your answers.

- Interview requests usually come with short notice when journalists are working on tight deadlines, especially with breaking or national news stories.

- Both phone and written responses to journalist questions require well-thought-out answers that are precise and meaningful in order to be included in an article.

By the Numbers: Print Demographics

- Traditional newspaper readership (i.e., for hard copy newspapers) is usually men and women aged forty-five or older.

- The variety of online publications is huge, and the age range is broad.

- Blogs are topic specific, and therefore have a targeted audience.

- Trade publications have a niche audience relative to their industry.

TELEVISION

What Makes Appearing as an In-Studio Guest on TV a Great Opportunity?

Television can also lend huge credibility to you as an authority in your field.

In addition, television has more sticking power today than ever before. Television, as with radio, used to be a fleeting experience, because once the interview aired, it was gone. Now, many news stations keep links to programs on their websites for a short period of time. You also want to obtain a digital copy to post on your own website, both to enhance your credibility and for the benefit of journalists and producers who may be vetting you for their own shows or publications. Nothing conveys credibility like an online video of you appearing as an expert guest on a TV show.

While TV audiences are harsh judges, you don't need to lose twenty or thirty pounds if you're overweight, or even change your hairstyle if you're not happy with your appearance. You will, however, want to know the basics of how to dress, including the best colors to wear, what jewelry is appropriate, and so on, along with the basics of how to sit and where to look when you go on set. It can also help if you come across to viewers as natural but also likeable. "Likeability" is a big factor in whether a TV interview is successful. These are all things we'll be covering in more detail later in the book.

What You Need to Know About TV Appearances

One disadvantage of TV is that it requires travel if you're looking for media coverage beyond your hometown. Also, you'll find that some cities have no TV shows with a format for guests. So, if television is your medium of choice, check on the TV opportunities in the cities you will be visiting before you make travel plans.

Another challenge with television is that guest interviews are short (typically two and a half to five minutes), so communicating your message succinctly is of paramount importance for successful TV appearances. It's also important to have a visual component that can immediately engage the audience and showcase your book, product, or service. Say you're a personal trainer; you could take the host through some easy, positive exercises. If you have a cookbook, you could do a cooking segment where the audience can see the ingredients and recipes come to life.

One of our clients, the American Veal Association, wanted us to get them national publicity for cooking with veal. Luckily, they had a famous chef as their spokesperson, and it was right around Memorial Day, so we decided to do a grilling segment around using veal at your cookout. *Fox & Friends* loved the idea and agreed to the interview segment. Because it was a national TV show, we brought in a professional food designer to make sure the presentation of the final product looked enticing to the viewers.

The segment was fabulous—and TV was exactly the right medium. It wasn't just an article in a magazine with some recipes. It wasn't just a conversation on the radio about how good veal is. When it was grilled before your eyes on live TV, you could almost smell and taste it. What better publicity could you ask for?

If you are likeable, caring, and look and sound professional, like our chef—and especially if you have an engaging visual presentation—nothing can compare to an audience seeing you on TV.

In-Studio Television Appearances: The Basics

- Interviews are typically two and a half to five minutes max.

- They should include visuals that support your message.

By the Numbers: TV Demographics

- Daytime TV talk shows tend to have a female or family-friendly audience, both locally and nationally. Think *Ellen*, *Oprah*, *The View*...

- National cable TV talk shows on networks like CNN, CNBC, and MSNBC are more focused on business topics.

RADIO

What Makes Being Interviewed on Talk Radio a Great Opportunity?

Perhaps no medium connects you as intimately to an audience as does talk radio, where eager listeners tune in to hear a favorite host chat with guests on topics ranging from politics to health care to finance and beyond.

"Talk radio is a major platform for people seeking publicity because it literally puts your message right in the mind of the listener," says my good friend Michael Harrison, founder and publisher of *Talkers Magazine*, the leading talk radio trade publication dubbed "The Bible of Talk Radio" by *Businessweek*. "Radio has a very dedicated audience, and they're paying attention. They are an active audience and a large audience. If you're trying to promote a brand, a product, a business, it's worth gold to be in front of them and introduced as an authority in your field."

Each year, *Talkers Magazine* profiles the talk radio listener, and every time, their survey confirms that the talk radio listener is "diverse, educated, attentive, active, and affluent." If this describes the listener you want, you've got a perfect match. And you can get even more specific with your target audience. Specialty talk shows on finance, law, politics, health, relationships, lifestyles, consumer advocacy, sports, gardening, and more allow you to identify shows whose audiences will be interested in your message.

If you're among the legions who listen to talk radio, you know how addicting the medium is, and how actively engaged its listeners are. It's a remarkably interactive relationship, more like friends talking to friends, which is why it represents such a strong third-party endorsement of you, your book, the product you may be selling, or your service. It organically builds authority for you and credibility for your business.

Since top hosts and their producers are businesspeople driven by merciless ratings, they are understandably picky about whom they interview. They only want guests and topics that will engage the audience and keep listeners tuned in, and that's good news for you: once you're being interviewed on a show, you can rest assured that you'll be talking to an extremely targeted audience.

Now that most stations are streaming live on the internet, talk radio interviews have even greater value. Alert your social network followers about when your interview will occur, and after the interview, post a link to the archived version or your own MP3, so that even more followers can tune in.

On talk radio, you also get enough time to tell your whole story. As a guest, you typically have ten to fifteen minutes of quality time to effectively convey your message to a targeted, attentive audience.

Finally, most talk radio interviews are done by phone; no need to travel to the station. You can have live conversations from your home or office with potential new clients or customers living anywhere around the country.

What You Need to Know About Talk Radio

AM radio is home to most talk shows, and it's where we book clients most often. FM stations are home to music, although we're seeing more and more FM stations incorporate talk shows into their format. There are also talk shows on Sirius XM, a subscription satellite radio service. In addition to tuning in on your radio, you can also listen on a station's website, where they often air their best shows.

The format and topics of talk radio shows will vary from morning to night. The morning commute is a great time to be on the air, as it's when the largest number of people listen. But don't discount overnight interviews. While you may think that no one listens to the radio at 3:00 a.m., overnight talk shows (midnight to 5:00 a.m.) are wildly popular with truckers, people who work graveyard shifts, public service employees, and others in twenty-four-hour industries.

Throughout the day, there are a huge variety of specialty talk radio shows on all sorts of topics—gardening shows, food shows, business and finance shows, lifestyle and health shows ... just about anything you can think of. We're also seeing more and more female-oriented shows on the radio. Whatever demographic you want to reach, whatever niche audience you want to engage, there's a talk radio show for that audience.

A Talk Radio Secret

Here's a little-known secret about talk radio: a large number of radio shows heard on the weekends are with hosts who buy the air time to have their own show. It's one of the most effective ways to become a recognized voice on the air and an authority in your field.

Here's a wonderful example of how this can be done successfully: I once caught a chiropractor's radio show when traveling across the state of Florida. He was a master. Listeners would call in with questions about their health, and he had the gift of sounding as if he and the caller were together in a private room in his clinic. He delivered his helpful advice with the most compassionate, caring manner.

The airwaves made him the ideal doctor—one who everyone wants at their bedside when they don't feel well. He would, of course, invite each caller to come to his office, making them feel that it was a special invitation. His office had to be flooded with new patients, week after week, from his own paid show.

Buying time on traditional radio stations isn't the only option. In fact, if you want to go national, one of the best ways to do that is to buy programming time on Sirius XM. I had my own national talk radio show on Sirius XM, and my cohost and I would get calls from all over the country.

If you're interested in purchasing radio time, here's an insider tip: Saturday morning is one of the best times for an hour-long program. Also important is what shows come before and after yours. Being sandwiched between good shows is a smart move. If the show before yours is really popular, more people are likely to stay tuned in as your show starts—and then, if your show is engaging, entertaining, and informative, you'll hook them in.

What About Podcasts?

Podcasts are very popular today, and they are continuing to grow. Why? Because anyone can have one—which is both good news and bad news. Many podcasts are truly excellent, and many are not. But the best of them trump being interviewed on terrestrial radio. People tune into podcasts because they have a strong interest in the topic of the show, so you're talking to a very targeted audience. Also, a podcast interview is often thirty minutes to an hour long, compared to radio interviews which average ten minutes, so you have more time to expand on your message and build rapport with listeners.

My advice is to do podcasts regardless of audience size. Frankly, it's great experience. Even if only ten people are listening, you get the chance to hone your message, experience the different questions a talk show host might ask, and refine your answers. And, at the end of the day, you don't know who's listening. One of those ten people could be someone important who could be a difference maker for you.

Talk Radio Interviews: The Basics

- Radio interviews today are all done by phone.

- Major market radio interviews are typically seven to ten minutes in length.

- Midsize market radio interviews can be ten to twenty minutes.

- Smaller market radio interviews can be thirty-plus minutes.

- If relative to breaking news, be prepared for interview requests within twenty-four hours. Otherwise, bookings are often scheduled two weeks out.

By the Numbers: Radio Demographics[4]

- Seventy-two percent of listeners are ages thirty-five to sixty-four.

- Seventy percent are college graduates or have attended college or graduate school.

- Men comprise 58 percent, women 42 percent of the listening audience.

- Sixty-nine percent earn $40,000 to $100,000-plus per year.

- Seventy-nine percent of those eligible to vote do so.

- Secular talk radio shows skew higher male than female.

- Religious talk radio shows skew higher female than male.

SOCIAL MEDIA

What Makes Social Media Great?

Traditional media outlets are a great way to build your brand and publicize yourself, but they stopped being the only game in town long ago. Social media sites have risen as an alternative means for reaching potentially millions of people.

Think of it this way: social media is the world's biggest cocktail party, and everyone is there—including your competitors and your potential customers. I first heard the cocktail party analogy from marketing guru David Meerman Scott, who used it in his bestseller, *The New Rules of Marketing & PR*. It's a great analogy that explains why social media networks are marketing gold.

---

4   "Talk Radio Research Project," *TALKERS Magazine*, accessed March 10, 2019, http://www.talkers.com/2011/10/27/talk-radio-research-project.

Let me set the scene: Imagine walking into a networking party at a hotel. People roam the room, engaging with folks they know and are introduced to those they don't. They talk about the economy, the weather, the latest movie sensation. You chat with someone, and he asks what you do for a living. In my case, I would say, "I've got a national PR company and we get our clients featured in the press and interviewed on radio and TV." The person might respond, "Wow, I've got a friend interested in that. Let me introduce you!"

Now, the friend may or may not be present at this cocktail party. But imagine that same conversation happening on a social network such as Facebook. That friend and possibly hundreds more would be so close by they actually could be "listening" to the conversation. Even if they're not actively following in real time, the conversation might appear in their news feed later.

That's what makes social media so valuable: you can be exposed to thousands more potential customers or readers than you would through traditional networking channels. That's because social media users stay connected by following each other. If I'm following you, I see your conversations. Post something clever and I might share it with my followers. If they like it, they might share it with their followers, and before long, you and your brilliance could be exposed to hundreds of thousands of strangers. Some will be intrigued enough to become your followers and soon you have a growing audience.

It's easier to get publicity if you have a "platform"—something that elevates you in the eyes of the media. Elected officials, by virtue of their office, have a platform, as do movie stars and champion athletes. Now, thanks to social media, the rest of us can have one too. Your thousands of followers create an attractive platform that tells journalists and show hosts that you not only have a built-in audience, but also a message that resounds with a lot of people.

We'll be talking more about all things social media in Chapter Seven.

By the Numbers: Social Media Demographics

The demographics of social media are wide ranging. I usually say that the demographic for social media is everyone! But demographics do differ from one platform to another. Here are some basics on four of the major platforms for adults in the United States who have internet access (which accounts for eight out of ten adults in the United States):[5]

- Facebook
  - Seventy-nine percent of adults with internet access use Facebook (eight out of ten adults in the United States have internet access).
  - Eighty-eight percent of eighteen to twenty-nine-year-olds, 84 percent of thirty to forty-nine-year-olds, 72 percent of fifty to sixty-four-year-olds, and 62 percent of sixty-five-year-olds (and older) use Facebook.
  - Eighty-three percent of women and 75 percent of men use Facebook.

- Instagram
  - Six hundred million active users.
  - Thirty-two percent of adults use Instagram.

---

5   "Social Media Demographics to Inform a Better Segmentation Strategy," Sprout Social, March 6, 2017, https://sproutsocial.com/insights/new-social-media-demographics/.

- Fifty-nine percent of eighteen to twenty-nine-year-olds, 33 percent of thirty to forty-nine-year-olds, 18 percent of fifty to sixty-four-year-olds, and 8 percent of sixty-five-year-olds (and older) use Instagram.

- Thirty-nine percent of women and 28 percent of men use Instagram.

- Twitter
  - Nearly 79 percent of Twitter accounts are outside the United States.

  - Thirty-six percent of eighteen to twenty-nine-year-olds, 23 percent of thirty to forty-nine-year-olds, 21 percent of fifty to sixty-four-year-olds, and 10 percent of sixty-five-plus year-olds use Twitter.

  - Twenty-five percent of women and 24 percent of men use Twitter.

- LinkedIn
  - Twenty-nine percent of adults use LinkedIn.

  - Thirty-four percent of eighteen to twenty-nine-year-olds, 33 percent of thirty to forty-nine-year-olds, 24 percent of fifty to sixty-four-year-olds, and 20 percent of sixty-five-year-olds (and older) use LinkedIn.

  - Thirty-one percent of men and 27 percent of women use LinkedIn.

In Print, TV, or Radio—Don't Dismiss the Small Guy

Some clients tell us, "I don't want to waste my time on shows in small markets or with small publications." We tell them that's a mistake. Small markets and small publications are anything but a waste of time.

Small towns throughout the country are blessed with daily or weekly newspapers that keep their communities informed about local news. While these more obscure practitioners of journalism admittedly lack some of the luster and renown that top-tier publications enjoy, they can be more important than you realize as you build your reputation as an authority in your field. Here's why:

People read their community publications. Weekly newspapers and small dailies still attract a loyal readership for one simple reason: they provide readers with articles that have a direct impact on their lives and keep them apprised of what's happening with people they know. If you want to promote your brand, it never hurts to start there. It can be a stepping stone to bigger things, plus you get to hone your interview skills in preparation for the day when *The New York Times* calls!

Smaller publications can have a bigger reach than you think. What happens in lesser-known media venues doesn't necessarily stay in lesser-known media venues. Story ideas that bubble up on the local level can get noticed at the national level. Many smaller newspapers are owned by large newspaper chains, and the publications within that chain share articles with each other, which means your interview with a newspaper in Sheboygan, Wisconsin, could be printed in sister publications far and wide. Not everything that grabs widespread attention begins life on the front page of *The New York Times*.

Journalists often write for more than one publication. Even if an article is for a small publication, you want to do the interview, because you never know whom you're talking to. Many publications now have articles written by contributors rather than staff writers, which means there are many writers out there who are writing for multiple publications, both small and large. The journalist who interviewed you for a small blog or a local paper may also be writing for *Fortune* or *Forbes*. If you give a great interview and develop a good rapport with the journalist, he or she may well ask you for an interview for an article they are writing for a big publication.

Much of this is true for radio and TV as well. Cities with smaller populations also have devoted fan bases, because listeners have fewer shows from which to choose. Not only do you talk to a loyal audience, it's also likely your interview will be longer than it would in a larger city, which gives you greater potential for making a strong impression and driving home your points.

And Remember: Media Follows Media

One piece of PR advice that I have shared with clients over the years is that they need to take advantage of every media opportunity they possibly can, no matter how big or small. Why? Because the media follow the media.

When you're trying to attract media attention to promote your brand, you may encounter what can be thought of as a media domino effect: one media opportunity leads directly to another media opportunity, much the way the toppling of one domino causes another to fall.

Members of the media routinely check what topics other members of the media are reporting about and whom they are using as sources. If they see that some other media outlet has made use of your expertise, they're more likely to view you as credible and someone they might want to turn to as an authority on your subject.

We experienced a terrific example of this phenomenon when one of our clients wrote an opinion piece we got published in the *New York Daily News*. After the piece appeared, our client was sitting down to dinner with his wife when his cell phone rang. On the line was someone from MSNBC, calling to check on whether he might be available to be interviewed for the network's *The Last Word with Lawrence O'Donnell*. The reason he made their list of potential guests? Someone at MSNBC had seen that *Daily News* article. The domino fell, and another media opportunity landed in our client's lap.

❖ ❖ ❖

As you can see, each medium has its advantages and disadvantages. Once you've determined who your target audience is and what your comfort zone is in terms of TV, radio, or print, you can then zero in on the best media fit for you.

CHAPTER FOUR

FIVE TACTICS FOR SUCCESSFULLY PITCHING THE MEDIA

Grabbing the media's attention isn't always easy. Each day, newspaper journalists and hosts and producers of TV and radio shows scroll through a never-ending barrage of email messages, many of which they delete without bothering to read. With competition for the media's attention so fierce, how do you separate yourself from the pack and land an interview that will help build your credibility as a go-to expert in your field?

It all goes back to what we talked about in Chapter Two: understanding the media's needs. The bridge between yourself and the infinite news media comes down to one thing: access. You must successfully access the media gatekeepers, interns, assistants, producers, and even the journalists or hosts themselves. In order to do this, you have to get inventive, allowing those creative juices to flow as you brainstorm alone or with others about pitches that might resonate with a show host or article angles that will intrigue an editor.

For example, one of our clients was willing to talk about Generation Z, which is the generation born from the mid-1990s to the early 2000s. We found that there seemed to be interest in how Gen Z fits into the workforce, a topic that would tie into both the client's message and their target audiences.

We crafted a short pitch promoting our client as a source who could speak on this topic. Nothing happened at first, but a couple of weeks later we got an email from a *Wall Street Journal* reporter saying that the idea fit perfectly into something she planned to develop into a larger, in-depth piece. Could we set up an interview with the client? Of course!

I learned early on that if you are useful to producers, news anchors, talk show hosts, and journalists—and you provide valuable information that will engage their audiences—they'll respond to your emails quicker and return your calls.

While no strategy for securing media coverage is foolproof, there are some approaches that will increase your odds of success.

Let me share five tactics we have used successfully over the years for pitching to the media:

1. Never pitch yourself.

2. Instead, pitch the ISSUE on which you're an expert.

3. Never pitch your company or the product or services you provide.

4. Instead, pitch the PROBLEM your company, product, or service solves.

5. Tie your topic to the news.

These five tactics aren't theoretical; we use them every day with our clients. For example, we had a pediatric endocrinologist client a few years ago wanting to publicize a new product he had developed for children with diabetes. We knew that we couldn't go out and simply pitch the product to the media, because they would just tell us to go buy advertising. Instead, we tied the topic to the news.

At the time, the obesity epidemic among American children was incredibly topical, with stories in the news almost every day—so that's what we focused on. We went out to the media with comments from a highly credentialed pediatric endocrinologist (our client), including tips on what parents could do to help their children who were prediabetic or obese. One of these tips was relative to our client's product and included a link to his website.

We didn't pitch our client. We didn't pitch his product. Instead, we had a great topical story, a spokesperson with impeccable credentials, and valuable information addressing the problem and proposing solutions for families with children suffering from obesity.

Successfully Employing the Five Tactics

How can you employ these tactics? What are the best ways to catch the media's eye? There are many specific tips for pitching the different types of media, which we will get into shortly, but first, here are a few vital things that will help you engage interest from the media you reach out to.

FIND YOUR UNIQUE MESSAGE

If there are a lot of people who do what you do, how can you set yourself apart so the media, and prospective customers, notice you? All of the ingredients are there, just below the surface—but if you're not looking, or don't know where to look, you'll miss them.

I'll give you an example. Some years ago, while on a business trip, I sat next to a man on the plane who glanced over my shoulder as I worked on notes for a speech, and he noticed that I was a publicist. Intrigued, he wanted to know what I could do for a guy like him. I learned he was a financial planner on his way to a marketing convention. I told him he needed to identify what special qualities set him apart from his competition and to develop that as his personal brand. He looked at me with a blank stare.

I began asking questions: What was his expertise? How would someone benefit if they hired him? He gave me his standard sales pitch, and I asked how he was different from other financial planners who would give me the exact same pitch. Did he have a particular client type he preferred? What was he passionate about in his work? He struggled to come up with answers.

Finally, I asked him if he read a lot about his industry. Yes, he said, every day. "What's on your nightstand right now?" I asked.

He lit up. "It's about IRAs and how baby boomers can leverage them most effectively. It's a topic I love." And there we had it—a topic that was both a passion and a strength. It was right there all along; he just hadn't seen it.

Unusual credentials can also make your message unique while adding to your credibility. We had a client who's a financial planner, psychotherapist, and artist. She focused on women's emotional responses to finances and how they can get in the way of making the best decisions. She was colorful, humorous, and compassionate— and her distinctive background gave her unique positioning.

One of my favorite examples of clients setting themselves apart involves three cardiologists who had all written books and had all come to us at the same time for help promoting their books and themselves as experts. One might think we would have to take turns representing them, since they were so similar, but fortunately the similarity was only skin-deep. One of the physicians—the one we mentioned in Chapter Three—was passionate about ways that people can protect their heart through their diet and lifestyle. His book focused on the Mediterranean diet as a heart-healthy way to eat. It also included recipes, exercises, vitamin recommendations, and more ways to live a healthier life.

The second cardiologist focused on end-of-life issues. He'd had the firsthand experience of having a near-fatal heart attack that brought him to the emergency room at the very hospital where he saw his own patients. As he didn't have his own end-of-life documents in place, he realized how important it was for people to have them. This became his passion, and he set up a foundation to spread the word on a national level.

The third cardiologist wanted to raise awareness about a simple test for detecting heart disease that doesn't involve invasive procedures. He recommends it to all of his patients because it leads to early diagnoses and treatment.

All three cardiologists could have written the same book with the same title along the lines of *How to Have a Healthy Heart.* Instead, each built their own platform from which they could speak on a unique angle they were passionate about in their shared field of health.

It's not always that easy, but by digging a little deeper and uncovering the spark that's firing your drive, you can begin to shape your unique message—it's what will make you stand out from others in your industry looking for that same media recognition.

Once you have identified your message, you can truly start utilizing the five tactics.

DON'T PITCH YOURSELF; PITCH THE ISSUE

The media hear from self-proclaimed "experts" all day long. They don't care about you; they care about how your expertise and your message will add value to the lives of their audiences. Don't write a pitch that says, "Want to interview the best fitness trainer in the state? That's me!" Instead, try something along the lines of: "Many people begin the New Year vowing to exercise more. I can provide your [readers, listeners, viewers] with tips on how to follow through on those resolutions."

Based on your profession or experience, what can you tell the media's audience that they will find valuable or interesting? Can you give them advice on how to take advantage of a change in tax laws? Can you help them navigate the growth of their business? Can you explain from personal experience how the foster care system can be improved? Here's the secret irony that I love so much about the media: when you're not actively trying to promote yourself, you can actually achieve a greater degree of self-promotion.

DON'T PITCH YOUR PRODUCT/SERVICE/ COMPANY; PITCH THE PROBLEM YOU SOLVE

If your pitch sounds like a commercial, the media have advertising departments they will happily put you in touch with. And if you go in talking about your company, product, service, and so on, the advertising department is exactly where they will transfer you.

The best article and talk show ideas are those that help solve a problem the readers or audiences face. People perk up when your message means something to them personally. Ask yourself: What are some of the problems my clients or customers are trying to solve? Those problems—and the solutions you can offer—can be the inspiration for a potential story pitch to the media. For example, a financial professional can offer tips on what to do if you haven't saved enough for retirement. A doctor can suggest ways to avoid becoming ill while on a cruise.

While the word "problem" carries the connotation of something heavy and serious, there are plenty of lighter "problems" that capture an audience's imagination just as strongly. A product we all had fun with was a gizmo that reminds men to put the toilet seat down. It's done with humor, but the entrepreneur says it actually trains most offenders within three weeks. Recognizing that the toilet seat is at the center of many a spousal tug-of-war, we offered up our client to talk about the "age-old gender power struggle" for a segment called "What's Up with the Toilet Seat Debate?" Since that was the inspiration for his creation, he had funny stories to share as well as some interesting insights about the ups and downs (so to speak) of married life. Talk show hosts recognized the potential for a lively and enter-taining conversation and snapped him up.

TIE YOUR TOPIC TO THE NEWS

If you want your pitch to get attention, the best way is to tie it to the news. You increase your chances of engaging the media's interest if your pitch aligns with something that people in the news business are already writing and talking about. They want fresh angles that their competitors don't have, and if you can provide that you'll be their new best friend.

You should begin each morning by checking out what's happening in the world. Google News is a good place to start for a nice menu of reports from a variety of news sources, but there are plenty of other places to look as well. What's going on that fits into your area of expertise? Are you a surgeon who can explain a new study involving your specialty? Are you a divorce lawyer who can comment on the latest celebrity split? One of our clients was a scientist who could talk about an eclipse that was in the news. We kept him very busy with radio interviews leading up to that astronomical event.

Sometimes the connection to a major news story is obvious. When Amazon announced that they were going to acquire Whole Foods, we knew exactly whom to call: our client who, as a global branding strategist, had been a key player in the turnaround of both McDonald's and Nissan. As soon as the Amazon news hit, we immediately reached out and told him that we wanted to offer his comments to the media on how consumers and customers would respond to the acquisition, and how it would affect the brands of Amazon, Whole Foods, and their competitors.

We reached out to top-tier press offering our global branding expert as an authority who could comment on this story. Within a couple of hours, we were setting up interviews for him with *USA Today*, the *Houston Chronicle*, CNBC News, and several other major publications. At five o'clock that same day, the *USA Today* article came out, and in the next day or two the same article came out in over two hundred other publications. Two weeks later, the story still had legs, and our client got an interview request from an Associated Press journalist for a follow-up story. That story came out in hundreds more publications.

Another client was a wealth manager in New York. When President Trump announced his new tax plan in January of 2018, we wrote an Associated Press-style article addressing the plan, quoting our client as an authority and offering three or four bullet points providing valuable information and advice about the plan.

Right away, we got a call from a *USA Today* journalist saying, "I loved the article. I'm actually doing a story on this; can we interview your client?" We set up the interview, and the story came out in their online edition at five o'clock that very evening, and in print the next morning. In the hard copy, the article was front page, and our client was quoted along with two other top wealth managers. The online version got picked up by a few hundred other publications.

You don't just have to look at political, economic, or business news to find your tie-in. It could come from something as left field as a celebrity meltdown. Many years ago, we had a client who was an anger management consultant and had written a book on the subject. About three weeks after she hired us, a story broke and became a national news sensation: you may remember the recordings of Mel Gibson's angry, anti-Semitic tirades.

It was the perfect tie-in—and it didn't end there. Around the same time, a JetBlue steward became furious at one of his passengers, and when the plane landed, he opened the emergency exit and slid down the inflated slide to exit the plane. That story became a national sensation as well.

We used these two national news stories as part of our headline to grab the media's attention, then followed up with comments from our credentialed expert on anger management. We didn't pitch our client; we addressed the problem these news stories focused on and had our client bring in solutions to that problem. Soon, our client was all over the radio, in the top-tier press, and getting calls from CNN and *The View*.

Why was our tactic for these clients so successful? Because we followed the news, tied our clients' expertise to it, and offered the media angles they could use along with a credentialed authority they could interview.

IF NOT THE NEWS, TIE YOUR PITCH TO SOMETHING TIMELY

While sometimes the news connection is obvious, other times it requires creative thinking. You can look beyond immediate news stories and consider other timely topics. You can plug into national holidays and special days, weeks, and months, just about all of which you can find on the internet. Own a hardware store? National Chimney Safety Week might be a good time to offer homeowners tips for getting their chimney ready for winter. If you own a preschool or other kid-oriented business, October 1 is Child Health Day. There's National Literacy Month, National Breast Cancer Awareness Month, National Smile Day, National Walnut Day … There's a special day for just about anything you can think of.

We have a client who specializes in diagnosing and treating halitosis and who has developed a number of products to address that problem. We've helped him stay in front of audiences for many years, with print and on radio and TV talk segment angles ranging from "National Fresh Breath Day" to "How Do You Tell Dad He Has Dog Breath?" (for Father's Day).

Beyond individual holidays, don't underestimate the draw of something related to the season. A company that emphasizes design in its production of innovative containers for plants wanted exposure in print publications. The CEO hoped those publications would also run photos of his eye-catching containers. We wrote a fall color trends article quoting the CEO and offering his tips for creating dramatic displays of color using container plants, subtly mentioning his own products by way of example. The article got picked up by a number of magazines—from trades to home décor—many of which included color photographs of the containers.

WHEN IS NOT THE TIME TO PITCH? WATCH THE NEWS

There are times when it might be better to back off from what's topical, such as during a national tragedy, a serious social issue, or a particularly intense political season. This doesn't mean you can't say anything. It's perfectly appropriate to express sadness over a national tragedy, for example. If you have legitimate expertise or advice to offer—such as a psychologist who can discuss how parents can talk with their children about a tragic event—then it makes perfect sense for you to get involved.

You want to avoid tying your product or service to bad news in a way that makes it look like you're trying to capitalize on some horrific event to increase sales. On social media, where you're directly reaching your target audience, you risk backlash, and your brand could be tarnished. With the traditional media, you risk damaging your relationship with those gatekeepers who might be less inclined the next time to pay attention to what you're pitching.

Even if you're not trying to tie your product or service to a tragic story, a big news story may still have an impact on your pitch in terms of timing. We put together a radio pitch for a dentist about the effects of drinking alcohol before bed. We thought it was a great topic and that we had a great pitch, and we were sure we'd get tons of interview requests. But we didn't get any responses.

We later realized we sent the pitch out right as Hurricane Florence was hitting. No wonder we didn't get a response—everyone was paralyzed by the storm. At that time, it was the only news story on which people were focused. Our pitch may have been great—but the timing was completely wrong.

If a big story is breaking either nationally or locally and your pitch is unrelated, wait until that breaking news is past. This is another reason it's important to follow the news: to know when it's the right time or the wrong time to send out your pitch.

Some Other Pitching 101 Tips

ALWAYS INCLUDE YOUR CREDENTIALS

You'll want to highlight your credentials when you reach out to the media. Otherwise, why should the media—and the media's audience—listen to you as an expert on your topic? However, make sure you keep it succinct. There's no need to dump your entire resume in the media's laps and bury them in irrelevant information. For example, if you are a financial expert, it is vital to know that you are a partner in your firm for nearly ten years, but it is inconsequential how many dogs you have, that you are passionate about windsurfing, that you worked in the restaurant industry for five years, and that you have a minor in advertising from BCU. The media is interested in your achievements. What are the things in your career that signal your credibility?

And here's a tip: don't be shy! People are often reticent to brag. Even the greatest experts in the world often don't like to tout their own success. But if you want to make it in the media, you're going to have to learn how to toot your own horn a little. In your bio, don't be self-effacing. Don't be humble. Go ahead and brag. Tell them your highest achievements and credentials. Position yourself as an expert, because that is how they want to identify you. They want to make you sound like the best thing since sliced bread, so let them know your credentials and why their audience should listen to you.

KEEP IT BRIEF AND SIMPLE

You have a lot to say about your topic, but you don't have to say it all in the media pitch. Print journalists and TV and radio show hosts don't have time to read a thesis, no matter how remarkable your insights are, so keep it succinct. Think of those pitches as a movie preview, not the feature presentation. You need to include enough information for them to get the gist of what you can talk about, but leave all those extraordinary and important details that you are tempted to cram into the pitch for the actual interview.

Along with including too much information, it can be tempting to get clever with your writing. While pitches and articles should be engaging and well written, don't get so carried away with creative language and clever phrasing that the message is lost in a forest of adjectives and adverbs. Resist trying to impress the media with how brilliant you are by stuffing in exotic words that will send them scurrying to the dictionary. They don't have the time or motivation to scurry. As Mark Twain put it: "Don't use a five-dollar word when a fifty-cent word will do."

DON'T FORGET THE IMPORTANT DETAILS

Along with the content, *make sure you include your contact information*! I can't emphasize enough the importance of having your contact information clearly visible and accurate. Don't weave it into your pitch, and don't rely on your recipient hitting the email reply button. Include a telephone number that you can answer at any time, or one for daytime and another for evenings and weekends. You may get just one call from the editor or producer interested in your pitch, and if you don't answer, he or she may very well move on.

Finally, your communication should be professional. Make sure your email is free of typos, grammatical errors, and other mistakes that make you appear less than professional. Never write a pitch and hit "send" without carefully rereading it to be sure it is clean, makes sense, and is as concise as possible. If there's no urgent need to send it immediately, give yourself twenty-four hours, then look it over again before sending.

ALWAYS LEAVE AN OPENING FOR SOMETHING MORE ...

Telling the media how they can utilize you gives you a much better shot than asking the media to think of how to use your expertise themselves. While suggesting a specific angle, it doesn't hurt to mention that you can also speak on other issues related to the topic and offer a few examples.

Writing and Distributing Your Pitches

If you turn to the back of this book, I've included an appendix of sample pitch formats if you aim to reach media nationwide. If you're after local publicity, here are some steps for how to approach the media in your hometown.

TALK RADIO PITCHES

If you normally listen to your favorite FM rock station or your music streaming device while you're driving around town, it's time for some new auditory scenery. Unplug the iPhone, push the AM button, and tune into the local talk radio shows. Who are the hosts? What's their subject matter? Do they have guests on the show, or is it just the host doing all the talking? If the host has guests, does the conversation cover things in your area of expertise? Which shows cover topics relative to your message? There are general format talk radio shows that cover a wide scope of topics, from news to sports to lifestyle, but there are also shows that focus on more specific topics: health shows, business shows, religious shows, cooking shows, gardening shows, etc.

If you want to know more about the shows you like or other shows airing on that station, visit the station's website. There, you'll find information about all the different shows that air, the show schedules, host's name, and contact information for the show's producer or host, all of which makes things extra easy. If contact information is not posted, call the station and ask how to reach the producer of the show you're interested in.

Many of the top-rated stations in a market will air national shows throughout the day, like Dave Ramsey or Sean Hannity. You want to look for the local shows that have guests, not these nationally syndicated programs. Unless you have built up a strong media resume, know that these national shows are a long shot. When you're starting out, it's better to aim for the local programs.

Once you've gotten the name and contact information for the producer or host, craft your email. Keep it short, friendly, and framed as a helpful offer rather than trying to sell yourself. You want to start with a good subject line so that they'll open up the email—maybe something like "Big fan." The opening line should reference that you listen to the show and are a fan, and want to introduce yourself because you've heard them talk about whatever your topic is. Let them know that you are a leading authority on that topic, with offices in the local community. Offer your time to come on the show as a guest and share valuable information that their audience would appreciate. You should include two or three suggestions of what you can talk about. Then, make sure you leave contact information. Include both your phone number and your website.

If you don't hear back within a week, I suggest following up with another email, referring them to your first one. You can mention that you know they receive so many emails, and you're resending yours just in case it got buried. If you still get no response, wait another week, then leave a phone message referring them to your email. Sometimes the friendly tone of your voice and the quality of your communication in your message will get them to call back. You can also try reversing the order: first an intro email, then a phone call, then a follow-up email. Be persistent but nice. And it always helps to mention something you heard on their show.

TELEVISION PITCHES

For TV, you can follow a similar process as for radio. Watch your morning network affiliate station shows (ABC, CBS, NBC, Fox) and see which morning or afternoon show has a format for guests. You can also go to the stations' individual websites and check out the shows there. Then, follow the very same formula as above, with the addition of including a visual aspect to your pitch. If, for example, you are the chef of a local restaurant, suggest preparing an interesting and easy meal on the air, showing the audience how it's done.

When you're pitching to local TV shows, make sure you mention that you're local. A show producer will choose you as a local expert over an out-of-town expert if your credentials are the same, because the producer can easily call you back on the show whenever the need arises—if you do a good job!

PRESS PITCHES

Many of the same rules as TV and radio apply when reaching out to the print media. If your reading time is spent mostly with magazines and books, then it's time to meet your hometown newspaper and other local publications. If you're not aware of other publications, look for them at newsstands and in news racks at shopping centers.

You can also search online for community news websites and blogs. Take note of the topics that particular reporters write about, and which editors are in charge of what sections. Check bylines to see if a specific reporter writes about your topic. If you're unsure, call the main newsroom number, tell them you want to submit a story idea on your topic, and ask who the best reporter or editor to send it to would be. The more you can tailor your pitch to an individual, the better your chances of getting his or her attention.

Once you've decided where to send your pitch, follow the same steps as for radio and TV. Start with an introductory email, making it clear in the subject line that you are local. Journalists receive emails from all over the country; yours will stand out if the subject line clues them in that you are from their community. End your pitch by saying that if they aren't interested in this particular story, you would be happy to be a source for any future articles they are working on that relate to your expertise.

As with television and radio, if you don't hear back, you can try sending another email a week later, and following up with a quick phone call to let them know you sent the email and are available for any questions. If you're sending a pitch for a specific article idea, I wouldn't send a third email; after two emails and a phone call, either they are interested or they aren't. At that point, it's probably time to come up with a new idea for an article to pitch them.

When it comes to print, you must understand newspaper and magazine timelines. Newspapers have tight deadlines, so if you have a hot news story, get it to the paper immediately or it's no longer "news." Magazines have a much longer lead time, with monthly publications often scheduling their issues three to six months ahead—so make sure you pitch your story far enough in advance to be one of the few selected.

Most major dailies have both national and international news. It's important to mention that you're local if the topic is a localized one. If it's a national news story being covered by your major daily local paper, you can offer your comment in two or three sentences so they can quote you without having to conduct an interview. Just make sure you reference your credentials in a brief sentence. The goal is to make their job easy by giving them good content for their articles that will interest their readers.

DON'T WAIT FOR AN INTERVIEW— GO AHEAD AND WRITE!

Don't underestimate the importance of having your writing out there. One of the best ways to do this is by having a blog or newsletter on your website. When journalists want to learn more about you before they schedule an interview, they will often go to your website and look for a blog to see your thought processes and ideas at work.

Another often overlooked means of getting publicity is to contribute articles you wrote to publications. Not only does your published byline boost your visibility, it provides an excellent credential for you as an authority.

While most major publications don't accept unsolicited articles, some do set aside space for contributor columns or accept guest columns on their op-ed pages. Smaller publications, trade magazines, and online publications are also good places for your articles to land, as these publications often have a small staff and are happy to get well-written articles that they don't have to pay for.

Here are some tips on submitting articles for publication:

Look for submission guidelines on the publication's website—and follow them. Some publications post their rules for submitting unsolicited articles. They may outline the topics they're interested in, minimum and maximum word counts, and the style. If you find guidelines, stick to them. The number one mistake people make is going over the maximum word count. That will very likely get your article rejected. And since editors often don't tell you why they're rejecting the article, you'll keep repeating the same mistake.

Pitch your ideas before writing a full article. While with some publications you can submit a full article, you can save yourself time if you first pitch a few ideas to gauge whether the editor would have any interest. Send a short email offering three or four topics, with a one-paragraph synopsis of each. By giving the editor several ideas for articles, you can increase your chances of success. Add a brief bio highlighting your relevant credentials.

Be prepared to offer exclusivity. Many publications state up front that they will accept only articles that have not been previously published. They may also require the writer to agree that they won't submit the article to other publications until a specified number of days pass. Or, the editor may tell you it's okay to publish in magazines that it doesn't directly compete with. Be sure to check the fine print.

Sign up for Google Alerts. Don't assume the editor will contact you to let you know when the article has actually been published. One of the best ways to track that is to sign up for Google Alerts so you'll be notified when the article is posted online. Once that happens, be sure to make a PDF of the article so you'll always have it in case the publication removes it from the website later.

Bylined articles help you establish your reputation as an expert, build your brand, and gain visibility. They may lead to an invitation to be a regular contributor, as has happened with a number of our clients. And bylined articles can generate even more interest from other publications whose editors see your work and may approach you wanting their own interview or story.

A Few Final Tips for Getting the Media's Attention

THE POWER OF EMAIL

Because of email, there is more opportunity than ever before to get yourself out there. Email levels the playing field, opening doors to all sorts of people most of us didn't have a prayer of reaching prior to the internet. The downside is that the ease of email means the media gets flooded with email pitches. If you can craft a brief, compelling subject line, which will at least get them to open your email, and then have a compelling headline so that they want to continue reading, and *then* your writing is clear and professional, you've gained the edge.

Because of the digital age, the media landscape is ever changing. Companies are operating with less staff than they did just five years ago. That means the producers and editors screening emails and pitches are much busier, moving more quickly, and far less patient. Therefore, your subject line is critical. It's the first thing producers and editors see—it needs to be intriguing enough to stop them in their tracks so that they don't pass you by.

Your subject line should be a sound bite conveying the relevance of your message in an engaging way. Ideally, it's just five or six words long—eight words maximum—so that it's visible in its entirety when someone looks at their inbox. You want the subject line to be a complete thought for the reader before they even open the email.

We have a client who wrote a book about responsible dental practice ownership, in which he talks about issues that can relate to any business. The headline for our pitch to radio shows was "Why are you so stressed out running your business?" The subject line for our email was "Is your business stressing you out?" Since we were pitching to business-focused radio shows, that subject would be sure to grab attention; business owners are almost always stressed out. On another pitch for a different client, we had the headline "Has social media become too big a risk for businesses?" For the email, we used the subject line "Why social media is risky business."

Of course, email isn't the be-all and end-all. When we don't get a response to our emails, we go the old-fashioned route: we pick up the phone and call. Those "old" techniques are sometimes still the best.

BE PERSISTENT—AND PATIENT

Sometimes media opportunities emerge quickly after you pitch journalists with a great story idea. Often, though—especially with the print media—those opportunities take time, and the fruits of your labor may not reveal themselves until days, weeks, or even months after you send out your pitch.

We experienced a remarkable example of this when a reporter for the *Atlanta Journal-Constitution* reached out to us with a surprising request. She wanted to speak with one of our clients about an article we wrote for her campaign that examined how to talk to parents who are grieving the loss of a child. We had written that pitch a year earlier, but the journalist remembered receiving it, searched her email, and there it was, ready to lead her back to us and our client. The interview went so well that our client was featured prominently in the article. Over the next several days other publications picked up the article, and a week later, that was still happening. It was a big win all around, all due to a year-old pitch.

If you haven't heard back about a pitch you sent out, you can certainly follow up, as we discussed earlier in this chapter. It's important to be persistent, but it's also important to be patient. Whether you like it or not, your timeline doesn't matter. The media's timeline does. While you may not be the person who fits into the article they're working on today, that could change tomorrow or next week—but only if they know about you.

Lastly, even if you score an interview with a major publication, that doesn't always mean an article quoting you will magically appear the next day. Some articles have quick turnarounds, but others might not see print for weeks or months, especially if it's a magazine article. Your capacity to accept delays may be pushed to the limits, but if you hang in there, the rewards could be just one more news cycle away.

That being said, just because you haven't heard back about your pitch doesn't mean you should stop pitching and do nothing. In fact, I'd advise you to keep trying. Be persistent. Even though one pitch failed to strike their fancy, the next one might strike publicity gold.

AND REMEMBER ...

Once you start booking interviews, keep track of the people who let you through the door. Make friends with the journalist; you never know what other publications they are writing for—and if you give them good content, they will think of you as a resource they can count on. The same holds true for radio and TV hosts and producers. Constantly add to your network of secretaries, assistants, producers, editors, talk show hosts, and even intern gatekeepers. Know whom to contact when it's time to remind them of your expertise.

❖ ❖ ❖

Keep making those connections, keep honing your unique message, keep finding those news stories, issues, and problems your expertise can address, keep writing and submitting those pitches— and before you know it, you'll be getting on the air and into the press, bringing your knowledge to the world and growing your brand as an authority in your field.

CHAPTER FIVE

TIPS FOR GIVING GREAT INTERVIEWS IN THE PRESS, ON RADIO, AND ON TV

You've booked a press, radio, or TV interview. Congratulations! Now you need to nail it.

Most celebrities appear casual on radio or TV and come across as eloquent and thoughtful in print. It looks easy, but it takes a lot of work to truly become comfortable in front of the cameras, behind a microphone, or when talking to a reporter. Even "naturals" need coaching on how to weave a story, deliver a fact, or convey their message so that they remain in a viewer's consciousness long after they've turned off the radio or TV, thrown away the newspaper, or logged off of the internet.

Some people assume they will be "natural" on the air because they're public speakers or teachers. I cringe when I hear this, because the rules of professional speaking don't apply when appearing as a guest on radio and TV. A public speaker who stands at a podium speaking to a group of people is in a structured environment. It's a one-way communication: speaker to audience. In this forum, a speaker has perhaps thirty minutes to an hour to convey their message.

Being interviewed by the media requires a very different skill set. As a guest on a radio or TV talk show, there is a two-way communication—you to the host and the host back to you, in a Q&A format. It's more entertaining to the audience to listen to a conversation than a monologue.

How do you become a good guest or a good interviewee? There are three simple tips that guarantee success across the board, whether you're being interviewed for radio, TV, or print:

1. **Be informative.**

2. **Be engaging.**

3. **Be inspiring.**

Interview Tip #1: Be Informative

Even the most entertaining guests might be seen as mere "filler" unless they actually have something worthwhile to say. Jokes, quips, and congeniality are all fine, but at the end of the day, radio and TV producers look for guests who are easy on the eyes and/or ears and are at the same time enlightening. The same is true for printed publications.

Playing the role of expert and doing it convincingly will help you build credibility with your audience—but be careful about trying too hard. Don't try to cram too much information into your limited interview time. You'll never get to relate *everything* you know (unless, of course, they ask you back a few times).

And here's another vital tip: leave the technical jargon at home. Don't assume the audience has the same knowledge as a crowd at an industry convention. Speak in a way the public can understand. Use layman's terms as much as possible and save the four-syllable words for your next Scrabble game.

The same goes for numbers and statistics. They're like verbal sleeping pills. If you have a special statistic that helps you hammer home your point, by all means use it. But be judicious; you're not speaking to a bunch of actuaries. Statistics and alert audiences rarely mix.

What you DO want to include is up-to-date information. Even passion won't carry the day if your information is old, stale, or unhelpful to the listener. You're the expert and you're expected to know the latest developments in your field. Why risk getting blindsided by a host who knows more than you do about your own industry? It's smart to dive into the news and check out your subject's major websites before you go on the air. Pay attention to research studies, surveys, the latest government statistics, and industry developments.

It also helps to go beyond just your industry or field. Knowledge IS power. Read your newspapers, either in print or online. Watch TV news. Listen to AM talk radio. What issues or news stories tie in with your business or message? Keep clippings and internet bookmarks updated with relevant stories from which to draw quotes, tidbits, and statistics.

Sound daunting? It's less so if you streamline your efforts. Find one or two websites that collect news on a wide variety of topics—finance, business, health, technology—to easily spot the top five headlines in each category. Check often. (We usually check Google News and *The New York Times,* among others.)

In addition to the most up-to-date national news, get local information whenever possible. If you're being interviewed on a talk show in St. Louis, go online and check out the *St. Louis Post-Dispatch* before the scheduled event. What stories tie into what you will be talking about? Do that in every market you appear in and you'll turn heads—people love it when you get local on them. You'll greatly increase the odds of keeping your audience tuned in.

This kind of research isn't just good for keeping up with the news—it's also vital in terms of understanding the show or publication before you get on the air or into the interview. Before going on, check out the show on the station's website. Look at other interviews the journalist has written up. You may learn something interesting about the host or journalist—something you can use in the interview. If nothing else, it's one less wild card you'll face.

This kind of research will also help you anticipate questions. Remember that list of brilliant questions for a host to ask you that you included in your pitch? When you land that interview, work on preparing succinct answers to each of those questions. These answers are your takeaways—the information you want the audience to take away from listening to the interview. For a talk radio interview, you can write those answers on a three-by-five card and have them in front of you. For a TV interview, you'll want to know them cold.

Of course, hosts can and will ask you whatever they please. In addition to having prepared answers to the questions in the pitch, try imagining what else you might be asked, then develop answers you're comfortable with.

Always be direct in answering questions. It's never wise to tap dance around an answer. Hosts want to keep their audience tuned in, and they'll shut you down if you don't help them. Give them an answer in a clever, direct way that funnels interest right back to your agenda.

And what do you do if someone asks a question to which you don't know the answer? Don't fake it. This is good life advice in general, but here I'm referring to fabricating answers to bewildering questions. If that happens, *just admit that you don't know* and move the conversation off that topic back to where you want it to go.

Lastly, no matter how many interviews you do or producers you befriend, make sure to involve your audience in the information you provide. It's your message, but listeners will only stay tuned if your message somehow applies to them.

Interview Tip #2: Be Engaging

We all love to be entertained. Even if your expertise is quantum physics, your appearances on radio and TV and even in print must be informative, educational, and, in a word, engaging. Be authentic, accessible, and likeable. Talk to your audience as you would to your family, coworkers, and friends, and you'll increase the likelihood that your audience will listen closely to what you have to say.

Every show is different, as is every audience. Some shows are serious, others are fun and snarky. Some are morning shows, others play late at night. Be enthusiastic and positive no matter what time of day it is and no matter whom you're talking to.

Your enthusiasm will be contagious. Your excitement about your message will radiate to the audience, and their excitement, in turn, will propel them to learn more about you and your book, product, or service after the interview. The insightful super salesman Zig Ziglar warned, "For every sale you miss because you're too enthusiastic, you will miss a hundred because you're not enthusiastic enough."

Here's a simple tip for upping your enthusiasm, even when you're on the radio and the audience can't see your face or body language: smile when you're on the air. Smiling gives your voice a more attractive tone. If you're smiling while you're talking, your voice sounds richer and happier—and listeners pick up on that. Conversely, if you're frowning, they'll pick up on that, too.

Be sure to match your attitude to your message. Ever see a newsman smile while reporting a horrible tragedy? I have. It doesn't mean he has no compassion; it just means he should have paid more attention to aligning his attitude to the circumstances. That's your challenge, too. You'll want to sound appropriate. If you have a positive message, act positive. If your message is about exercise and physical health, look healthy. If you're talking about a serious, upsetting subject, be appropriately somber. And so on. When audiences perceive your voice and/or appearance to be consistent with the topic, they're more likely to buy into what you're saying.

Audiences are also more likely to be swayed by what you're saying if you are confident. Confidence is the lifeblood of success. If you're not that confident about working with the media yet, take a page from Arsenio Hall's vast treasury of life quotes: "I don't possess a lot of self-confidence. I'm an actor, so I simply act confident every time I hit the stage." Whether confidence comes naturally or whether you merely pretend that it does, it's one quality that will make your audience want to listen to you further and want to do business with you. Confidence allows you to put yourself at ease and be yourself, which betters your odds of being a success.

Part of that ease will come from being conversational with your host. Speak to the host as you would to an old friend. This signals to your audience that you are friendly, approachable, and relaxed; someone they would want to work with or take advice from. Next time you talk to a friend, assign a part of your brain to pay close attention. Listen to the way you speak—to the volume, speed, humor, and "graciousness" (or lack thereof). Then overlay it onto your next interview.

Interview Tip #3: Inspire with Your Message

Above all, you must be a cheerleader for your message.

One of my earliest clients actually became my client just because he and his message were so inspiring.

It happened one Sunday morning as I headed to the store to buy some bagels and lox, a traditional Jewish Sunday morning breakfast. My car radio was tuned to a talk station when I heard a man talking about "the ten foods you should never eat." Although I was intrigued with the topic, I was mostly happy to hear an entertaining conversation while driving to the supermarket. But soon it was no longer merely entertaining conversation—I was absolutely riveted to the show and couldn't leave the car until I heard about every one of the ten foods I shouldn't eat. He convinced me that my health depended on it.

An incredibly entertaining storyteller, he was also a highly cre-dentialed and educated nutritionist. His message was informative and so inspiring that I stayed tuned in for the entire show (and was late getting home to my hungry family). I rushed to call his office on Monday to buy his book—and that's how he eventually became a client.

By the way, this nutritionist didn't just talk about the ill effects of sugar, cake, and candy. He created a nutritional urgency, one as important as any financial urgency. When he talked, he injected you with the need to know what the top ten foods are that you should never eat and why you shouldn't eat them. And then you'd also want his book and tapes to help keep you healthy, as well as his products to overcome the ill effects of consuming these bad foods your entire life. This compelling guest made the most of every interview—and he made a fortune selling products from his talk radio appearances.

Part of urgency is enthusiasm. As I said, enthusiasm is conta-gious, so be sure you bring lots of it to the table—hosts and journal-ists love it when you do. When you're excited about your message, it can't help but radiate to the listeners or viewers of the show.

You can help propel your audience by ending each interview with a "call to action." This is not a pitch or a hard sell. You don't want to sound like an infomercial. It's just telling people how they can learn more about the topic you're discussing. Hopefully, you'll be so informative and approachable in the interview that if somebody hears you on the radio or sees you on TV, they'll want to learn more.

❊ ❊ ❊

While these three tips are true across the board, each medium also has its own specific needs. Here's some advice on how to give the best interviews in each medium.

Tips for Being a Great Radio and TV Guest

GET TO THE POINT—AND STICK TO IT

In today's information-driven world of talk radio, talk TV, news-papers, magazines, blogs, e-zines, and newsletters, fast information is what people want. Who has the time or interest to sift through meandering comments or fuzzy dialogue to capture the essence of your message? It's important to keep your message short and clear. People want to hear what you have to say, but they don't have all day to figure it out.

Tune in to any drive-time radio talk show or morning guest spot on the local TV channels and you'll hear plenty of sound bites: short phrases or sentences that capture the essence of the guest's message. Remember "Houston, we have a problem" from the great movie *Apollo 13*? That's a sound bite! Or those famous words uttered by former President George H. W. Bush: "Read my lips: no new taxes." Both short phrases clearly captured the essence of the speaker's message, and they're great examples of how you can capture the essence of your message.

Sound bites have gotten a bad rap. No sooner was the term invented than it got associated with the shallow and the insincere. Owing to the way the human mind works, sound bites are a smart idea. While listeners may not remember a paragraph of stuff you said, one of your sound bites may stick in their head, and that can cue them to remember the rest of your details. Sound bites act like callouts in an article, so have a few prepared.

This by no means implies that you should sound like an auto bot and repeat your well-rehearsed sound bite no matter the question, controversy, debate, or situation. Know what your key message is, then tailor it to match the moment. Know the key points you want to communicate and try to anticipate additional questions a host may ask you.

Know where the host's questions might take you. Always steer your answers back to your own key message and all will be well. It can be easy to get so wrapped up in talking with the host, and with the intoxication of speaking to tens of thousands of listeners *simultaneously*, that you completely forget to deliver your main message.

Notes are essential—but you don't want to read them on the air. It's always best to know your material cold. Reading notes—reading anything on the air, for that matter—always sounds stiff and rehearsed, which is a turnoff for your audience. On the other hand, notes can keep your presentation flowing and thorough. Read them to get the idea, then express that idea in as natural and spontaneous a way as you can. Remember, this is supposed to be friend-to-friend communication.

ENGAGE THE HOST

When I came out with my book *Celebritize Yourself* several years ago, my staff booked a lot of interviews for me. I was fortunate to get a little media coaching from a good friend, Lee Habeeb, a national talk show host himself who cocreated *The Laura Ingraham Show*.

One particular piece of Lee's wisdom proved especially helpful. "Don't worry about engaging the audience," he said. "That's the host's job! The audience regularly tunes in to the show, so the host already has engaged them. They aren't your concern." My job, Lee continued, was to engage one person and one person only: the host.

How can you prepare to really engage a host? To start, research the show. Listen to or watch a few previous shows to get a feel for what kind of show it is, the rhythm of the show, and how it's structured. This is easy to do today, because so many shows are archived online.

Then learn about the host. Who is this person who will be interviewing you? Find out everything you can. A good starting point might be the host's bio on the show's website, but you can also look up articles about them. What are their likes and dislikes? What about family? Hobbies?

Years ago, I was on a book tour with a client who was a very high-ranking government official. We were on our way to an interview with national talk show host Don Imus, someone my client knew nothing about. In the taxi, my client pulled out several pages of notes his staff had prepared about Imus. By the time we arrived, he knew about Imus's brother, his dog, and other tidbits of information that helped him win over the acerbic host and his audience in the process.

Once the interview begins, be aware of what kind of emotion the host is bringing to the conversation and try to match that energy. If you follow the host's tone, he or she will naturally have a positive reaction to you. If the host takes a very serious approach, you should respond in an equally serious manner. If the host expresses excitement for your topic, your voice should display similar excitement. Is the host jovial? Then you should be, too. If your tone is out of sync with the host, you will disengage the audience because the host will become disengaged.

Although these tips are about engaging a radio or TV show host, they can also be used if you're preparing for an interview with a journalist for a print publication. Research the types of articles the journalist typically writes and find out whatever you can about the journalist's background. Then, as with broadcast hosts, mirror that journalist's tone. Are they in a hurry because of a deadline? Then be succinct with your answers. Are they more laid back because they are working on a feature story or a long-range project and have more time? Then you can feel free to elaborate.

Engage the host—or the journalist—and the audience will take care of itself.

GET THE TECHNICAL SIDE RIGHT

Having a high-quality interview is also a matter of making sure the technical quality of the interview is high. For TV, most of those elements are controlled for you, because the interviews take place at the TV studio. For radio and podcasts, most interviews are done by phone, so the ball is in your court to make sure you sound as professional as you are.

The good news about phone interviews is that you get to do your talking in comfortable, familiar surroundings. The bad news is, well, you get to do your talking in comfortable, familiar surroundings— in other words, places where there could be barking dogs, meowing cats, noisy kids, and blaring TVs. So be sure you've eliminated, temporarily at least, any potential distractions. Turn off your computer and the TV and make sure you switch off your cell phone. Put the pets outside. Alert your family about what you're doing. Do whatever you have to do to stay focused.

Also, make sure you are ready to go on the air when the time comes. To be safe, call a few minutes early, and if the station is scheduled to call you, stay near the phone and keep other people in the house off the line.

Speaking of phones: try your best to use a landline. Cell phones are unreliable for on-air interviews. You can imagine how frustrating it would be to you and the host if your cell phone cuts out in the middle of the interview. Then there are issues of static and poor reception. All told, cell phones are far from the best option for talk radio interviews.

The same goes for speaker phones. This is all about broadcast quality, and speaker phones simply don't deliver. If you sound like you're talking from inside an echo chamber, chances are your interview will be cut short. Instead, it's best to use the audio horse-power that a hands-free telephone headset can give you.

MASTER YOUR SPEECH

Sounding professional—and engaging—is not just about the equipment; it's also about how you speak. Practice saying your main points aloud before your interview, and don't be afraid to get animated. Remember that it's not only *what* you say, but *how* you say it that counts. Good inflection keeps your listeners tuned in.

Also, while on the air, slow your speech down a bit and say your words a little more carefully. You never want to mush sentences together. On the radio you don't have the benefit of appearance or body language going for you—only your voice. If you speak too quickly or too sloppily, your listeners will have to work too hard to understand you and you'll lose your audience.

Another thing that can help you find the right tone and tenor is mimicking the host. It's a variation of an old sales/body-language secret: gently mimic your prospect. Since you can't scratch your chin when your host is scratching his, mimic other clues. How fast is your host talking? Is he or she slowing down, getting thought-ful? Or speeding up to sneak in a few more words before a com-mercial? Whatever the host does, take the cue and do the same. If you're in sync with your host's rhythm, your audience will enjoy the great rapport.

Finally, don't get hung up on mistakes. If you stumble, stutter, or otherwise slip up during an interview, let it go and move on. Everyone makes mistakes, so don't dwell on yours. You'll notice that TV anchors rarely beat themselves up when they flub a line—and you shouldn't either. Just keep rolling, stay "on message," and you'll be fine.

BE CIVIL—AND STAY CIVIL

It always counts to be polite. Simple things like remembering first names goes a long way. Most of us like being called by name—it's a sign of recognition and respect—so use that principle in your interview. Burn the host's first name into your brain and say it a lot. It probably goes without saying, but it's a cardinal sin to forget who the host is.

Take the time to hear and understand the host's questions and comments. Both host and audience will appreciate if you don't just talk, but also listen.

WHEN IT COMES TO TV, DON'T FORGET THE VISUALS

Remember that TV shows communicate to their audience visually as well as conversationally. One trick in developing your compelling "visual" is to ask how you would explain your message to a child. What pictures would best translate it into graphics for a TV story?

Here's an example: One client had a successful term life insurance agency, and we had to get very creative to come up with interesting visuals for his TV interviews.

Since the audience on daytime TV is mostly female, we had him talk about the mortality rate of men versus women. We created a graph that showed that women tend to live longer than men. Our client had a simple message: if women are living longer, they need to be financially prepared to take care of their families. And life insurance was a good solution.

Part of the visual for a TV interview is, of course, you. Be mindful of how you dress and sit. For clothing, it's best to dress in solids rather than patterns that may be distracting. Color-wise, avoid white or green (blue is a good go-to color), and avoid looking directly into the camera—keep your focus on the host.

ASSUME THE CAMERA AND/ OR MIC ARE ALWAYS ON

Always, *always* assume that the camera and/or mic are on. You may think they've stopped rolling, but things could still be live, or they could have turned the mic or camera back on without you realizing. Don't say or do anything you don't want broadcast to the world.

AND FINALLY, GIVE YOURSELF A BREAK

Every interview is a learning experience—an audition for the next interview. This doesn't mean you can treat them sloppily or show up unprepared, but give yourself a break. Actors have it easy; someone else writes their lines. Not only must you write your own sound bites, you must also make them up on the fly. Don't worry, you'll soon get the hang of it. It just takes practice and honing your communication skills—and getting comfortable being interviewed.

TIPS TO MAKE THE MOST OF INTERVIEWS WITH THE PRESS

IT'S NOT AS DIFFERENT FROM TV AND RADIO AS YOU MIGHT THINK

The premise for print media is the same as for TV and radio: they need informative and engaging material to keep their readers reading. Many of the tips above apply to a press interview as well, but here are some press-specific tips that will help you give an effective print interview.

BE TIME SENSITIVE

When you get an interview request, make sure you respond right away. Journalists are often on tight deadlines, so if you can't provide them what they need quickly, or if you can't fit their interview request into your schedule, they'll find someone else who can.

Once the interview is scheduled, don't be late. If you don't show up (or answer the phone) on time, you're risking that they will move on to another source.

Be respectful of the journalist's time in the interview as well. You should stick to the point and give succinct, well-thought-out answers so you make the best use of the journalist's limited time—and yours.

The value of being time sensitive is that, with any luck, you can build a relationship with this person and become a regular source for them on your topic.

MAKE YOUR COMMENT A KEEPER

On occasion, I hear people say they don't want to be part of an article that quotes others. They want to be the sole source. That might happen with a smaller publication, but don't expect it with top-tier publications. Most newspapers and magazines actually have editorial policy that requires they quote at least two to three people in every article. Being a part of the article is valuable regardless of whether you are the sole source. You're offering insight and possibly giving your opinion, but you are also getting the added bonus of an implied endorsement from that top-tier publication.

You should also know that the comments you give in an interview may never get to press. On one occasion, a journalist we work with at *Forbes* was writing an article giving financial advice for whoever wins the lottery, and came to us asking for quotes from three or four different financial professionals. We scrambled and got four of our clients to provide quotes—but in the end, only two of those quotes were used. We don't know why the other two weren't used, but I can tell you it was probably because they either weren't original enough or weren't engaging, or both.

Often, different experts will say similar things. The journalists are only going to pick the quotes that are the most interesting, the most well put, the clearest, and the most insightful. That's how they keep their readers reading.

How can your quote be the one that makes the cut? Journalists usually have a hard limit on how long their article can be, so they are looking for quotes that are well expressed and concise. You could make a brilliant, important point, but if your quote requires an extra paragraph to explain what you're talking about, it's probably not going to make it into the article. Even if the point you're making is the same as their other sources, the easier it is for the journalist to pull a clear, succinct quote from their conversation with you, the more likely it is that you will be the expert quoted.

If you're concerned that the journalist might get something wrong because you left out the full explanation for brevity's sake, send an email after the interview to sum up and clarify what you said. Be diplomatic. Instead of telling the journalist you were afraid they didn't grasp what you said, put the onus on yourself by saying you aren't sure you did a good job of explaining your points, so you wanted to provide the information in writing to help the journalist out.

While brevity is essential, the best thing is to give a quote that is not only brief, but unique. You want your answers to be distinctively you—to offer a new and engaging perspective, not just the same everyday information that everybody else is going to provide. If you give trite or bland answers to a reporter's questions, there's a good chance you won't make the cut. That doesn't mean you should exaggerate or try to get too clever, but you'll have an edge if you're capable of delivering a colorful quote or one that reflects your personality while still giving useful advice.

Ultimately, though, the most important thing is to convey information that's relevant to the angle the reporter is writing about. Journalists want information that their audiences can make good use of, not vague comments that provide no help to them.

❈ ❈ ❈

Practice, Practice, Practice

For TV, radio, and print, practice makes perfect. Pull out your cell phone and record a mock TV appearance. How do you look? Do you appear comfortable? Friendly? Defensive? Is that red shirt your best color? Does that tie match that shirt? Are your shoes clean and polished? Do your clothes fit well? Are they clean and pressed? These may seem like insignificant details, but how you look represents something very significant: a first impression.

Do the same for radio interviews. Record yourself and listen to how you sound. Are you speaking clearly, or mushing all your words together? Do you sound excited and engaging, or are you speaking in a monotone?

You can also go back and watch or listen to interviews you've already done, to see where you can improve. Go back and read your press appearances as well to make sure you expressed your message clearly. I know that watching yourself being interviewed on TV or listening to yourself on the radio can be rather painful. My advice? Do it anyway. It's a vital step. Grit your teeth and listen to or watch yourself over and over again. I promise that if you make critiquing a habit, you'll improve your game twice as fast as you otherwise would.

If you think about it, every interview is a new opportunity. The more interviews you do, the better guest you'll be.

Honesty Is the Best Policy

Finally, and perhaps most importantly: be honest. While I'm sure you wouldn't outright lie about something, you might be tempted to exaggerate while in the throes of telling a good story. But the whole point of your publicity effort is to build your credibility, so if it's something that can be easily found out, it will undermine everything you're trying to accomplish.

Part of being honest is also being honest about yourself. Don't respond to a journalist's question using six-syllable words when you're used to talking in everyday language. The real unprocessed "you" communicates a lot about your character, and that gives audiences a better handle on both you and your message.

❖ ❖ ❖

This is a lot of information I've shared about giving good interviews, but don't be intimidated. You have the credentials, the knowledge, and the expertise. By following these tips, along with just being you, it won't take long until you've mastered the art of the interview and can share your valuable message with the world and become one of the media's go-to experts.

CHAPTER SIX

HOW TO LEVERAGE MEDIA COVERAGE TO BUILD YOUR BRAND AS AN EXPERT

You've pitched the media and you've landed some great interviews on the radio or TV or in the press. You aced the interviews and now have some great media appearances to add to your credentials. But the process isn't over yet. You've made a great effort getting the media to notice you, but if it all ends there, you've wasted a lot of time and energy.

Promotion is actually a two-step process. Step one: Get your message heard. You're on the air and in the news, people see you, hear you, read about you, and like what you have to say. They're motivated by your message and want to learn more. Accomplish this first step and you're on the way to building your brand as an authority—but you won't get anywhere without step two.

What's step two? Leverage that publicity. If the information you provided in the interview is truly valuable and helpful to a listener or viewer or reader, they will want to reach out to you and work with you. Make sure you give them a way to do that; otherwise it's all for naught and you're getting only a small fraction of its value. It's up to you to use your publicity as a critical part of your marketing to let people know these implicit endorsements exist.

The impact of even one TV appearance or quote in a national publication can be multiplied many times over. So, let's talk about how to get the most out of your media coverage.

Eight Tips to Leverage Your Media Coverage

Leveraging your publicity into something more than a "here today, gone tomorrow" moment is a matter of thinking outside the box and not being shy about promoting yourself. Here are eight ways to do this:

#1. INCORPORATE IT INTO YOUR SALES AND MARKETING MATERIALS

Share links to some of your best coverage in your online marketing material and be sure to use it in flyers, brochures, direct mail advertising, and other promotions. Incorporate the logos of the major press you've appeared in, with highlighted quotes from the articles, into all your sales and marketing materials.

One of our clients in the financial industry took this tactic and ran with it—with stellar results.

Like many financial professionals, he hosted dinner seminars for prospective clients. We did a media campaign for him, and got him quoted in notable publications like *Bloomberg*, *USA Today*, *Investor's Business Daily*, and other top-tier national media. After this campaign, he incorporated his publicity into all of his sales and marketing material and included it on the dinner-seminar invitations. He was able to legitimately say, "As featured in *The Wall Street Journal*, *USA Today*, and *Bloomberg*." If you received a dinner invitation like that, and then an invitation from another financial professional vying for your business but with none of these credentials, it's pretty clear which seminar you would choose to attend.

His strategy worked. You can imagine that people thought, "If those publications are quoting him as an authority, he's the guy I want to listen to." But our client didn't stop there. At the seminars, he erected a big pop-up stand displaying the logos of those publications and the quotes from the articles. Everyone who walked into the room could immediately see that they were talking to a noted financial authority. All of this substantially increased attendance at his dinner seminars, the number of clients he works with, and the total assets he now has under management.

#2. FORWARD COPIES OF PRINT ARTICLES TO CLIENTS TO REINFORCE THEIR CONFIDENCE IN HIRING YOU

Since almost all publications are now digitized, it's easy to email the link for an article to your clients. They will be happy, because that publicity validates their choice. They will be proud to say their attorney, for example, was quoted as an expert in *The Wall Street Journal* or *New York Times*. They will want to share it with everybody, to boast that they have the best in the business, further spreading the word about your expertise.

#3. SHARE THOSE ARTICLES WITH PROSPECTIVE CLIENTS TO ENCOURAGE THEM TO HIRE YOU

Sharing your media coverage may be the difference between a prospective client choosing you to work with over someone else.

We got one of our clients, a female financial advisor, quoted in some top news outlets—including Fox News. One day, she met with a married couple in her office to discuss managing their portfolio. The wife was excited about hiring her, because she felt that a woman would understand her needs. But the husband was more standoffish. He was throwing out question after question, situation after situation, testing our client, the advisor, on how she would handle things.

Finally, he asked her about a particular scenario, and she said, "You know, rather than me telling you how I would handle it, why don't I send you the Fox News article in which I was quoted on this very situation you've asked me about. Go home, read it at your leisure, and then you can come back and tell me how you feel about it."

"No, no," he said, pulling out his phone. "Let me see it now." She directed him to the article, and as soon as he saw that she had indeed been quoted in Fox News, he said, "All right. Let's start. How do we come on board?" That implied endorsement convinced him that she was the real deal.

#4. TALK IT UP! SPEAK ABOUT THE MEDIA INTERVIEW AND COVERAGE TO CLIENTS AND PROSPECTS—TO EVERYONE!

In the right setting, just the fact that you've been interviewed can carry as much weight as the interview itself. To get this point across, I tell new clients a story about a client we worked with. My office called him because we had a *New York Times* journalist wanting to interview him the next day at 1:00 p.m. Our client's answer? "I'm sorry. I can't do it. I'm in a meeting with clients at that time."

I got on the phone with him right away and here is what I suggested: "When your clients come in for their appointment, you say, 'Joe, Liz, I hope you don't mind, but in about half an hour I've got a journalist from *The New York Times* calling to interview me. Is it okay if I take the call? I will only be about ten minutes.' Of course, your clients will be impressed and happy to let you take the call."

Recently, I shared this story with a new client, and he started laughing. "Of course," he said. "Of course, I would take that call. But I love that story. And you know what? Even if I've got a big prospective client in my office, I'm going to tell him I have to take that call with *The New York Times* journalist!"

This new client also had his own radio show. "You should do the same thing on your show," I told him. "If we've booked an interview with a big-name publication, mention it on the air. Say, 'You know, when I was being interviewed by the *New York Times* yesterday …' That will build up your brand as an authority to your listeners even more."

#5. CREATE A "WALL OF FAME" IN YOUR OFFICE FOR ALL YOUR VISITORS TO SEE

Even if an article is only online, it's easy to have a graphic designer format it so it can be nicely printed and framed. Just make sure the logo or header of the publication is visible. When a client (or a prospective client) is sitting in your waiting room, there's nothing more impressive than seeing all the articles in which you've been quoted hung up on the wall. It gives them a guarantee of your expertise, and they'll walk in to meet with you assured that you're a trusted and respected authority in your field. That assurance is worth its weight in gold.

#6. USE IT TO BUILD YOUR BRAND AS A PROFESSIONAL SPEAKER

You should also incorporate your publicity in the marketing materials for your speaker business. Building your authority through coverage in national media is an effective way to stand out from the sea of professional speakers vying for the same speaking opportunities. After all, the more important you are, the better it makes the organization look to have you as a speaker.

Additionally, you can leverage your publicity to increase your speaking fees. The more national media you have, the more you're positioned as a trusted authority—and the more money corporations and organizations will be willing to pay for your expertise. Your value increases dramatically as a result of that positioning and media recognition.

#7. POST IT ON YOUR WEBSITE

Just like with your office, when someone visits your website, you want to give them an immediate assurance of your authority and expertise. If you're interviewed by a newspaper or magazine, make a TV appearance, or are a guest on talk radio, proudly share it for website visitors to see. It's a good idea to create a special "In the News" page that's easily accessible from your home page, and prominently display your endorsements: "As seen on CBS," "Featured in the *Chicago Tribune*," "Heard on WGN radio," and so on. This has the same effect as those framed articles in your waiting room: it lets visitors know immediately that you are a trusted and respected authority in your field.

#8. SHARE IT ON SOCIAL MEDIA

Social media is one of the absolute best ways to leverage your appearances in print, radio, and TV. If you're scoring PR hits with the traditional media, then Facebook, Twitter, LinkedIn, and other social media platforms become a great way to let everyone know about it. You might share those appearances through email, but your audience will be limited to the names on your mailing list. Share the news on social media and you will quickly extend your reach, possibly many times over. Anyone who reads your post can potentially share it with their followers—and those people can potentially share it with theirs.

Also, if you're booking media appearances across the country, social media gives you the opportunity to show everyone that your influence isn't limited by geography. Maybe you're a financial professional in West Virginia who's been interviewed on a talk radio show in New York or Chicago; that's going to be impressive when you share it with clients and potential clients on social media. If people elsewhere in the country are interested in what you have to say, maybe they should be as well.

But social media can be used for so much more than just leveraging appearances in traditional media. It's a force on its own, and it can be one of your greatest allies when it comes to building your brand as an expert—which is why I've dedicated the whole next chapter to using social media effectively.

❉ ❉ ❉

Put all of your media successes to work for you. Each medium you've appeared in has its own reach, but you don't have to be limited to just the immediate audience that saw or heard your message. By sharing those media appearances through email, on your website, on social media, at speaking events, and on the walls of your office, your success will be multiplied many times over.

CHAPTER SEVEN
MASTERING THE ART OF SOCIAL MEDIA PR

'm a huge proponent of using social media to market your brand—and of using social media PR. Because we're a publicity agency that also delivers social media services to our clients, it was natural for us to incorporate PR components into our social media activities. We developed this niche of social media PR without realizing we were doing anything different—until other marketing companies started to come to us and say, "We do social media marketing, but we want to hire you because our clients want PR and we're not a PR agency."

Return on Networking— The ROI of Social Media PR

You may be asking what the difference is between social media marketing and social media PR. The answer is that they both try to influence the conversation and spread the message about a brand; they just do it in different ways. Social media marketing is more about trying to elicit some sort of instant action by a customer or potential client. For example, you can buy advertising on social media platforms, or promote a sale or sweepstakes event, and then measure success by how many people buy your product or sign on as a client as a direct result. The goal of social media PR, on the other hand, is long-term brand building rather than instant sales. It isn't about a quick return on investment; it's a long-term relationship.

What's the return on investment, the ROI, for putting that kind of time into social media PR? I can tell you from personal experience that the "return on networking" (RON), as it is called, is huge. With all my social media accounts combined, I have somewhere in the neighborhood of 130,000 friends, followers, and connections. They expose my name, business, and message to their audiences every time they "like" one of my posts or share one of my links. Let me offer just one example: One time, a person retweeted something I'd posted on Twitter—and that person happened to have 150,000 followers. That's a potential audience of 150,000 people I might not have reached otherwise. Talk about exposure!

People interested in what you have to offer may follow you on social media even though they have no immediate plans to sign on as a client, but that doesn't mean you're not reaching them. Social media is similar to a billboard. Like the effects of a billboard, the RON of social media isn't always immediately tangible. All those people see your posts again and again—like drivers passing a billboard. If your content is engaging and your message valuable, when the time comes to do business, you're the one who comes to mind—just like the company with the billboard that sticks in drivers' minds.

By establishing a continued presence online through regularly sharing content that is useful to your followers, you build your platform and your reputation as an expert. That grows in surprising ways—and it lives in surprising places.

A case in point: I once received a call from a prominent New York City hair stylist, the director of a salon in one of the city's premier department stores. He wanted to talk about his publicity needs and what my firm could do to help him. When I asked how he got my name, he explained he'd written some books over the years with a coauthor, and she had heard me at a speaking engagement. Well, that made sense. Speaking at conferences is a great way to get your name out while also building credibility. But the next thing he said came as a surprise.

"So, then I contacted the corporate office of the department store chain and asked what PR agency they would recommend. They said, 'Marsha Friedman of News & Experts—we heard she's the best.'" I may love to shop, but I don't know a soul in the corporate offices of that high-end retail chain. The only possible way they could have heard "she's the best" was through social media.

The RON of social media PR includes increased traffic to your website, increased trust in your brand and what you're selling, and greater word of mouth than you could ever hope for in the non-virtual world. Here are some more benefits.

BUILD RELATIONSHIPS AND STRENGTHEN YOUR CREDIBILITY WITH THE MEDIA

Social media PR helps build relationships with traditional media. Since social media marketers are more intent on driving sales, they aren't likely to engage in much interaction with news reporters. But social media PR is a great way to engage with journalists and bloggers who routinely write about your area of expertise. You can comment on things they post or ask them questions, and that inter-action can increase the odds that they will turn to you when they need a source for an article. You'll never get to establish that sort of interaction if you're simply paying for social media advertising or posting preordained content.

Having a strong social media presence can also help establish your credibility. If you get on the media's radar, one of the first things they'll do is Google your name or your company's name and check out your presence on social media. You want them to be impressed with what they find. The greater your following and the more exciting your content, the more intriguing you'll appear. A large, built-in following makes you an asset to the media—or, simply put, the more popular you are, the more valuable you are as a guest or interview subject.

At that point, the whole situation can become self-perpetuating. A growing audience can help lead to media attention. Media attention can help grow your audience. It's a delicious cycle!

TEST OUT NEW IDEAS

Social media PR gives you opportunities to test media outreach and provides a great forum for launching new ideas. If your feedback from your followers is positive, you could then pitch that idea to the media to get mainstream coverage or use it in your advertising campaigns. For example, we helped one client establish a good level of social media engagement with her content about blockchain, which we were then able to turn into pitches to send to print media, which led to coverage in top-tier publications. Then we linked to those print articles on her social media, so it came full circle.

BUILD YOUR PERSONAL BRAND

Social media PR also allows you to focus on growing your personal brand as much as the company's brand. These days, it's a good idea for a CEO or business owner to have a personal brand as well. It speaks to your credibility as a CEO, which reflects on the credibility of your company. People like to know who they are supporting, so using social media to influence the public's perception of you is important.

BUILD YOUR SOCIAL PROOF

Your social media following sometimes grows even more because of what's referred to as "social proof." Social proof is simply the phenomenon that when we see others taking part in an activity, we're more likely to be drawn to that activity ourselves. We go to see a blockbuster movie because everyone we know seems to be going to see that blockbuster movie. The perceived popularity becomes "proof" of its quality or value. Likewise, in the world of social media, when people see that you have hundreds or thousands of followers, they tend to perceive you as trustworthy and are more likely to follow you as well. In short, as much as we might like to claim otherwise, we really are influenced to a large degree by our peers.

❊ ❊ ❊

Clearly, the benefits of social media cannot be overstated. So, how do you make your social media the best it can be? Here are some tips, strategies, and tactics to help you build, use, and maintain your social media presence and take full advantage of all the benefits social media PR has to offer.

Start with Your Website

I cannot overemphasize the importance of your website. After all, what's one of the first things you do when you want to learn more about a new store that opened in town or to research a financial professional a friend recommended? If you're like me, you go in search of their website. People do the same thing on social media: if someone finds your Facebook page or Twitter or Instagram and wants to know more, they'll go to your website. You don't want someone who was engaged and intrigued by your social media presence to hit a dead end when they get to your site.

A well-designed, well-organized website is essential. It can build an incredibly valuable database of people who are interested in you, so that you can interact with them directly and stay in front of them on an ongoing basis. It can help you tell people what sets you apart from your competitors. And it can go a long way in emphasizing and upholding your brand as an authority.

Making Social Media Work

Once your website is set up and ready to go, it's time to turn to all those social media platforms: Facebook, Twitter, Instagram, LinkedIn … where do you even start?

Remember that cocktail party analogy I used for social media back in Chapter Three? Generally speaking, what works when you're networking at a conference are the same approaches that work on social media.

Go in with a plan. If you're going to a party to network, you have goals. Maybe you want to find prospective clients or get people interested in your upcoming project. You identify your target demographics and learn which influencers will be at the party—the local media, politicians, celebrities, and so on. On social media, the world's *biggest* cocktail party, making the right moves gets a bit more complicated and involves some strategizing, but the concept is the same, just on a larger scale.

Don't stand in the middle of the room saying the same thing over and over. Repeatedly posting the same message, such as "Come in for our big sale tomorrow" or "We won Business of the Year," is like going to a party and saying the same thing over and over. Instead, engage in conversations on a variety of topics. They can relate to your business or book, but in a tangential way. If you sell jewelry, for instance, share a great trick for cleaning rings.

Be genuine and show personality. At a party, you smile and ask people questions about themselves. You may tell a joke or two, if that's your personality and the personality you want your brand to reflect. In the same way, let your humanity shine on social media, but don't pretend to be something you're not.

Build Your Following

Nothing that you do on social media matters if nobody is following you. Building an extensive social media following and making the best use of it is not only smart, it's essential if you want to take advantage of the marketing and branding opportunities that social media present.

Making connections with strangers is easier with some social media platforms than others, but here are some general strategies you can use:

- **Look for "influencers."** Find the reporters, editors, talk show hosts, bloggers, and so on who are likely to have an interest in your message, then post interesting content and mention them using their appropriate social media handle. If your company produces handbags, for instance, you might search Twitter for "fashion bloggers" and get a list of bloggers and their handles.

- **Search for keywords relevant to you.** These searches will turn up people with an expressed interest in your subject area. So, if your handbag company produces purses made from recycled materials, some keywords might be "fashion," "handbags," "recycling," "sustainable," or "women's accessories." Check out the resulting list of profiles and, if they look like people who could be interested in your products, follow or engage with them through a like or a comment. They likely will follow you back.

- **Follow the followers of others in your industry.** Despite what you may see others doing, don't try to "sell" these followers on your company or book. Simply add to the interesting dialogues relevant to your industry or target audience by sharing witty observations or insightful information.

Of course, if you're starting fresh, you can begin to build your base by inviting friends and family to follow you on any social media platform. But your family and friends are not the only resource available to you. You can also:

- **Make use of current contacts.** You probably already have an email list of clients or customers, plus people who have expressed an interest in what you have to offer. You may also have a newsletter list. Send an email encouraging these people to follow you on social media. They'll be able to share your tweets, Facebook posts, and other social media activity with their friends and followers, helping you expand your connections and spread your message.

- **Incorporate social media into other promotional activities.** When visitors come to your office or when you have a booth or speak at seminars, let people know how to connect with you on Facebook, Twitter, Instagram, or wherever else you may reside in the social media universe. If you do public speaking, add a frame to your PowerPoint that includes your social media information, such as your Twitter handle. And make sure to include your social media information on any business cards or brochures you hand out.

- **Make use of social media ads.** For a relatively small amount of money, you can take advantage of advertising on social media to grow your following. Social media ads can be used to laser target the consumers most likely to be interested in what you have to offer, helping you to find people you otherwise might not have connected with.

As you start gathering followers, you can continue to grow your following by posting content that is relevant and interesting to your target audience. You should also engage with that community or audience by liking their posts, retweeting, commenting, or sharing, which gets you in front of them in a subtle way and increases the chances of them following you.

You can also start adding and following individuals who fall within your target audience in an effort to get them to follow you back. Try to maintain a higher ratio of people following you than the number of people you follow.

A Follower Is So Much More Than Just a Follower

The value of growing a large group of followers goes far beyond just that group. When you're sharing with your followers, you're sharing with people who are interested in you and your topic. They're not random or bought; they're people who are engaged by your message, so they're going to share things you share with their followers. Then those people can share it with their followers, and so on.

If you have relatively few followers, but some of those followers happen to be big influencers, they could have very broad reach. Ideally one or more of your followers who shares your post has a large following of their own, in which case the number of people who see your post will exponentially increase.

The same thing is true for "likes." People tend to think of likes this way: "I got 112 likes!" And they think that's the end of it—but it's not. When someone likes your Facebook page, for example, their friends see it. And if a big influencer likes your page or post, even better.

In fact, much of what you do on social media has a greater reach than your immediate circle of followers, because they can share your posts and tweets with their friends, who can share it with theirs. And if someone comments on your posts or asks a question, their friends will see that, too.

And it doesn't stop there. There's impact beyond the internet as well. People discuss what they saw on social media at backyard barbecues, baby showers, cocktail parties, and just about any other place where they gather to chat. The more followers you have, the more people will be talking about you in the real world.

Hashing Out Hashtags

A great way to reach even more people is hashtags—that now ubiquitous symbol that looks like this: #. When you're on a social media site, you're trying to become part of a conversation. The hashtag allows people who don't follow you to find your contributions to that conversation. Without a hashtag, a lot of eyes that could have viewed your content never do.

For example, if you are on Twitter and tweet something without a hashtag, only your followers see it. If you use a hashtag, anybody who looks up that hashtag could see your post, and your post is now tied to every post that uses that hashtag. A hashtag paired with a common word, such as #love, can position your post to potentially be seen by millions.

Here are three ways to make the most of hashtags:

1. **Use branded hashtags.** One of the advantages of using a branded hashtag—such as #Ind500 or #DCcomics— is that it can help link people to a conversation around your brand, event, book promotion, etc. These don't get as much use as a generic hashtag, but the goal is to brand yourself through the hashtag with the hope it could gain popular use or even go viral.

2. **Don't overdo it.** A post littered with too many hashtags can be difficult to read or appear spammy. Twitter suggests using no more than two to three hashtags per post.

3. **Think geographically.** If you're aiming for local recognition, a hashtag that links to your location works well. Hashtags such as #Seattle or #Bangor drop you into numerous conversations about your hometown.

A hashtag may not look like much, but it's a powerful tool that's also a double-edged sword. If used correctly, it can bolster your marketing reach. However, used incorrectly, hashtags can have major unintended consequences.

For example, you may remember a few years back when one careless tweet caused a scandal for DiGiorno, the frozen pizza company. DiGiorno had noticed a trending hashtag—#WhyIStayed—and decided to take advantage of the moment by tweeting: "#whyistayed You had pizza." Unbeknownst to the pizza company, that hashtag was about domestic violence. The tweet couldn't have been more inappropriate, and as soon as the brand realized the mistake, their tweet was deleted and an apology appeared in its place.

These are important cautionary tales, but don't let them scare you off hashtags. Just do your research. If you see a trending hashtag that on the surface appears to be a good fit for your brand, make sure it means what you think it means before you use it!

All those hashtags floating around in social media land provide opportunities for you to increase the reach of your brand's message and bring on even more followers. Just make sure you know what you're attaching yourself to.

Stop and Think

One of the advantages of social media is that anyone can open an account and start spreading whatever it is they have to say—for good or ill. There's no barrier to entry in social media as there is with getting past the gatekeeper, editor, or producer who determines whether you are interviewed in the press or on the air.

But this freedom comes with its own dangers, beyond even using an inappropriate hashtag. It's so easy to sit down with your laptop or your phone, whip out a tweet about whatever pops into your head, and post it for all the world to read. If you scroll through social media platforms, you will see plenty of people doing just that, apparently with little or no reflection. That may be fine for personal use, but when you have a brand to promote—and to protect—it's best to stop and think before you post something on any social media platform.

Try to anticipate what, if any, negative reactions there might be and whether that's something you can live with. Ask yourself: Is the reward potential greater than the risk potential?

Almost always, with offensive or inappropriate material, the answer is no. You can ruin years of goodwill in an instant if your social media sites are used to post something that many people find offensive. You would think that's easy enough to avoid, but sometimes it might not be clear to you that a particular post or tweet could strike people the wrong way, so be careful out there.

Consider Your Audience

Your audience can and should influence all of your social media content. Knowing the likes and needs of your target audience will help determine the type of content you share on social media.

The social media platforms you choose should be based on whom you're trying to reach. Although there is overlap, each social media platform attracts niche audiences that may or may not be useful to your brand. For example, Instagram might be the right choice for you if you're promoting a lifestyle product to millennials and Gen Xers. If you are in search of baby boomers, Facebook would be a good place to look, because that's far and away their favorite social media platform. (Take a look at those demographics in Chapter Three if you need a reminder.)

Social media sites are all different, and you need to approach them differently. Facebook, for example, is the most consumer friendly and is the first place most people go, whether they want to share photos of their grandchildren or learn what others have to say about their experiences with a business. It also allows room for more detailed messages. LinkedIn is better for business and professional purposes. Twitter, with its character limit on messages, is the high-speed, information-now site, so it's a great place to check news updates. You also can get away with posting more often there than you can on other sites.

Whatever platform you're on, understand that social media is not one-size-fits-all messaging.

Leverage That Media!

In order to make the most of sharing your publicity on social media, you need to make people want to click on your link, to "like" it, comment on it, and/or share it. Unfortunately, many people don't think about that critical step when they share their publicity. I see a lot of posts like these: "Read the story about me that ran in today's *Gadfly Gazette*!" Or "'Like' my radio interview!"

Here are some effective ways to grab people's interest and get them to actually read your posts and click on the links to that great article or TV segment:

- **Use a nugget of information from the article or interview to show its value.** A fun fact, helpful tip or other information will help your post stand out and will do more to get readers to click on your link. A business-woman who's been interviewed about the growing number of female US business leaders might post, "The number of women-owned businesses in this country is growing 1.5 times faster than the national average! Here's why."

- **Ask a question that's answered in the link you're sharing.** Say you're a financial advisor who was interviewed about retirement planning for forty-somethings. Your post might read, "What are the four things you should be doing for retirement while you're in your forties?"

- **Share a photo or video.** Some social networks are very visual. A photo from the article or broadcast, or a photo or video relevant to the content, will attract more eyes than text alone.

You don't have to wait until the interview is published to start capitalizing on it. Go on Facebook, Twitter, or other social media sites to let people know the interview happened. You can do this in a way that doesn't sound (too much) like bragging, such as: "Had a great interview about retirement tips with a *Forbes* writer today. I'll let you know when her article appears!" As simply as that, you've shown your followers that you're a go-to expert for the media.

And once you've shared the article or interview, you don't have to stop there. If something comes up in the news relative to the article's topic, you can always share it again, even if it's months later. You can link to the article all over again, perhaps with a quick comment such as "I still can't believe all the positive responses I've gotten over the last month because of this."

Posting your media appearances is a good opportunity to interact with your followers, so engage with your audience, especially when it comes to positive responses or questions.

You can also use your social media networks to cross-promote anytime you're featured in traditional media. If you're getting booked as a guest on talk radio, for instance, promote the upcoming shows on social media, then visit the stations' websites for links to their Twitter accounts and Facebook pages. Join their networks, friend their friends, and plug the upcoming shows there, too. You'll make new connections from among the stations' listeners, which certainly won't hurt the next time you pitch them an interview idea.

Once the article or interview is out, don't forget to tag the publication or show and the journalist or host who interviewed you—they'll love the publicity as well. It will engage their interest in you even more and help develop a relationship.

If the publication or show shares a link to the article or interview, you can "like" or "favorite" the post or tweet. You can comment on it with a simple statement, possibly aimed at the writer, such as "Thanks for the great interview." By joining this conversation, you may pick up more social media followers or inspire some people to search out your website to learn more about you and what you have to offer.

Keep It Current and Active

Social media PR capitalizes on current events. A well-run social media PR effort aims to be relevant, tying the message to news, trends, or other things people are talking about right now.

A social media campaign is also always an ongoing effort. You can't take the view that you'll tweet for a week or a month and never have to engage anyone on social media ever again. It simply doesn't work that way.

The key to making social media really work for you is consistency. Stay active in your networks. Post often and wisely and pay attention to your followers. Your social media platforms need tender, daily care, because once you've grabbed your audience's attention, you don't want to lose it.

In order to do this effectively, you want to have a strategy for your content. Develop a stream of content that will be relevant and valuable to the right individuals through the right channels. Variety is also important. Your content should be a mixture of links, images, videos, and articles.

Stay abreast of trending topics and discussions that your target audience will find relevant, and become part of these discussions using valuable content, making use of trending hashtags when possible to demonstrate your professional expertise and drive people to your website. Take care to make your posts short and interesting, and if your content links back to your website, tease the information that will be available once they click through to encourage better click-through rates.

Along with consistently posting, make sure you're consistently interacting. When people comment on your post, ask you a question, or take the initiative to share something with you, respond!

Finally, remember when you're posting to keep in mind your audience's first question: "What's in it for me?" If the content you're sharing is mostly pleas to "Visit my blog!" or "Check out my wonderful homemade soaps," the answer is "Nothing." Find the message or benefit that speaks to the public and use it to shape your interactions.

You Don't Have to Go It Alone!

I wholeheartedly believe in the power of social media PR. I've seen what it's done to build my business and my personal brands.

It's been successful for me because I have a team of experts who take care of my social media—and when I have questions about social media, they are the ones I turn to.

If you're like me, an already busy professional, you might find it difficult to handle your brand's social media on your own and do it well. This isn't something you can squeeze in when you get a couple of minutes between staff meetings and phone calls with clients. A well-managed social media campaign is a long-term commitment, not a one-and-done deal. It takes strategy and skills unique to this medium, plus time and single-mindedness to build a valuable following and solidify your brand on these platforms.

❖ ❖ ❖

This is the relevance of social media PR. Once you have success with your social media and your PR, you want to capitalize on the inherent connection between these two marketing strategies. When used in harmony, they complement each other in an extraordinary way that increases the visibility of your brand and you as an authority in your field.

CHAPTER EIGHT

WHY PR IS A UNIQUELY PERFECT MARKETING STRATEGY FOR WOMEN IN BUSINESS

Whether you're a woman or a man, it's important to understand that we live in an opportune time for women in business. Women have some advantages in using PR to build their brand, and understanding this information will empower men as well in their marketing efforts. Things are incredibly different now than when I was growing up, and my experiences as a girl, a young woman, and a female entrepreneur have given me the perspective to see just how great things are for women today compared to how they were in times past.

When I was growing up, my brother was the one who was encouraged to get a college degree and have a professional career. My dad's dream was for him to become a chiropractor, so my parents were thrilled when my brother announced that it was his dream too. They were willing to sacrifice whatever was needed to send him to college.

My life, as the daughter, was a completely different story. When I said to my father, "Dad, I want to go to college. I want to become a social worker," my dad's response was "Sweetheart, no. You're a woman. Your job is to find a doctor or lawyer or other rich professional, get married, have children, and be a good homemaker."

I loved my dad; he was very special in my life—and I don't blame him for this response. In fact, before he passed away, I used to tease him about it. I knew that in his and my mom's generation, that's simply how things were. Women were wives, mothers, and homemakers. It was the man's job to work and bring home the money. The message was clear: careers were for men; homemaking was for women.

When I was a young adult, that started to change. I came of age in the midst of the women's liberation movement of the 1960s and 1970s, when women were starting to find their own voice. And in a way, my dad's response is what pushed me to find my own voice and my own path. It was the best advice he ever gave me, because it made me realize that if I wanted to do anything in life, I would have to do it myself. I couldn't depend on others—even my parents—to make things happen for me.

As it turned out, I didn't go to college, but I didn't choose to be a homemaker either. Instead, I chose to have both a career and a family. The week after I graduated high school, I went into Manhattan for a job interview, got the job, and never looked back.

For many years I worked for companies small and large, but eventually I decided to go into business myself. It was after I'd had success building my company that my mom gave me one of the biggest surprises of my life, just a week or two before she passed away. She knew she was dying, and in a real heart-to-heart conversation, she told me she'd always admired my path in life and my career. She told me she'd never felt like she had a choice. So she was incredibly proud that I hadn't settled, that I had made my mark as a woman in business. Anytime I had my picture in a newspaper or other publication, she would clip it out and keep it. When I had my own national radio show, she tuned in regularly. And when I published my first book, she gave it out to all of her friends.

My journey to becoming a career woman, wife, and mother isn't unique. The feminist movement caused many women to become dissatisfied with their limited options. Economic concerns also gave women more reason to enter the workplace, as inflation caused the cost of goods to rise to the point where most families with children needed two incomes. More women embarked on careers and were accepted in the workplace in roles beyond just being a secretary. Today we live in a different world, with women making strong inroads into areas long dominated by men, including top-level positions in business and politics.

All of these societal shifts mean that today there are more women in business than ever before. In fact, the growth and success of women-owned businesses is one of the most profound changes taking place in the business world—something bestselling author Margaret Heffernan wrote about in her book *Women on Top: How Women Entrepreneurs Are Rewriting the Rules of Business Success*. According to her research, between 1997 and 2004, privately held women-owned businesses grew at twice the rate of all other US firms. By 2008 (when the book was published), 40 percent of all privately held US firms were owned or controlled by women. That's 10.4 million firms. And every day in America, 420 new women-owned businesses are formed. [6]

Why are so many women starting their own businesses? Heffernan writes, "The single reason most often cited by women to explain why they go into business for themselves is simple: they want independence. They seek control of their own destiny. They don't want to be passive victims of corporations and strategies and men who don't value them."[7]

Not only are women starting their own businesses, they're finding great success doing so. Heffernan makes the point that because women take such great risks, women entrepreneurs have a much greater drive to succeed.

This is certainly how I felt when I started my business. I didn't have a particularly horrible experience in corporate America; I just intuitively knew it wasn't for me. Perhaps that was my father's influence; he was an entrepreneur, and I've realized that his entrepreneurial blood runs through me.

---

6   Margaret Heffernan, *Women on Top: How Women Entrepreneurs Are Rewriting the Rules of Business Success*, Reprint edition (New York: Penguin Books, 2008).

7   Ibid.

I started my first business at twenty-one, a coffee house in Venice Beach, California. This wasn't just a place to grab a beverage and a snack. It was a true Greenwich Village-style coffee house, with an open stage for performances from poetry readings to bands playing their original music. It was a wonderful place, and I loved the experience of owning and operating it.

Several years later, when I moved to Florida and got a job working for somebody else, I found it didn't excite me the way running my own business had. So when I finally launched my current publicity agency in 1990, I was a happy girl. Despite the long days, late nights, and weekends toiling away, I was elated, because it was my own business and I was working hard for *me*, not for someone else.

Then 9/11 happened. In the aftermath, the industry my business primarily served at that time—the natural health industry—took a dive along with the whole economy. As a result, my business started to tank. Revenue dropped, and I was facing bankruptcy and a debt of hundreds of thousands of dollars in undelivered services.

I couldn't live with the idea of closing the business and writing it all off as bad debt. Along with that, I knew if I shut the business down, there was the question of what I would do to earn a living. In that state of mind, I didn't ever want to launch another business, so the only option would be to work for someone else again.

I spent days in pure agony pondering those two options. When I visualized what it would look and feel like to work for someone else, I knew that option would be far too painful for me.

There was only one solution: I had to figure out how to turn my company around.

It took courage, endurance, and perseverance, but I knew I couldn't go back, so I had no choice but to go forward.

The need many women have today to leave corporate America and strike out on their own evokes feelings similar to what I had experienced.

❖ ❖ ❖

What does this all mean for your PR efforts?

First, it means that women today are a more important audience to target as customers than ever before. Second, there are more women in key roles as TV anchors and journalists. They enjoy interviewing women who are experts, because women bring a different point of view to the table.

Let's go more in-depth on these two points.

Overall, 40 percent of households are now headed by women.[8] Along with being the breadwinners and heading households, women make up the majority of consumers. Best-selling author Tom Peters has written a great deal about the power of women in business and has compiled information from numerous sources to show just how influential women are. Women make more than 80 percent of all consumer purchases in this country and hold over 50 percent of purchasing officer positions in companies. In other words, women are making the majority of both personal and commercial purchasing decisions.[9]

Women are not just the majority purchasers; they are the majority, period, making up 51 percent of the population, according to the

---

8   Léa Rose Emery, "40 Percent of Households Are Now Headed by Women," *Brides*, April 16, 2018, https://www.brides.com/ story/40-percent-of-households-are-now-headed-by-women.

9   Tom Peters, "Women BUY! Women RULE!," May 29, 2014, https:// tompeters.com/wp-content/uploads/2014/02/Women_buy-rule_052914.pdf.

US Census Bureau.[10] Because women are both the majority popula-tion and the majority purchasers, you want to be sure to include the women in your audience as you think about your message. After all, that's certainly what people in the media do. As the media monetize their business by ad rates primarily, they often play to women, since that's the audience their advertisers are interested in reaching.

In addition, women are a great audience to target because they are referral machines, as marketing guru Marti Barletta has written about in her book *Marketing to Women: How to Increase Your Share of the World's Largest Market*. Women tend to be more empathetic, caring, and nurturing, and enjoy sharing good things to help their friends and family. If a man goes to a great doctor, he's probably not going to tell all his friends about it. If a woman goes to a great doctor, she'll promote that doctor like crazy, sharing him or her with her friends, recommending that they see the same doctor.

Women get together for coffee. We get together for lunches. We share ideas. When a woman compliments another woman on an item of clothing, the automatic response is "Thank you! I got it from this or that store!" It's a natural instinct. So, if you want your brand as an expert to spread by word of mouth, women are the audience you want to reach.

Now Is the Best Time for Women to Have a Voice in the Media

Everything we've talked about in this chapter points to one important conclusion: now is a uniquely perfect moment to be a woman seeking national media coverage. Since the media depend on the dollars they

---

10   "Age and Sex Composition in the United States: 2016," US Census Bureau, accessed November 18, 2018, https://www.census.gov/data/tables/2016/demo/age-and-sex/2016-age-sex-composition.html.

receive from advertisers for their very existence, they play to women, and that means women have an advantage when it comes to seeking publicity.

We've seen the effects of this phenomenon when we send story ideas to our media contacts. Along with the story ideas, we'll give them a choice of experts they can interview, and when we include a woman, she is always their first choice. Why?

WOMEN BRING A DIFFERENT POINT OF VIEW TO THE TABLE

Everyone has experiences that shaped them, but women are more likely to have had experiences in line with the female majority of consumers. One example is a client we had who was a financial professional. She put an emphasis on helping women with their retirement, because she understood at the most personal level what it means for women to have a longer life expectancy than men, increasing the odds they will outlive their money and need long-term care. Because of her financial expertise in working with women on their financial plans for retirement, the media loved her, and we got her featured in such top-tier publications as *USA Today* and *Money*.

Even if the topic is not specific to women, women will have a different take on things than men. Especially in fields that have been long dominated by men, women are going to bring a new perspective—and as we discussed in Chapter Five, a different perspective is exactly what the media seek.

FEMALE JOURNALISTS AND TV ANCHORS ARE ON THE RISE—AND THEY WANT TO TALK TO WOMEN

Just as the number of women in many other fields is increasing, so is the number of women in prominent positions in the media. While men still make up the majority of journalists, the number of women journalists has been steadily increasing in television, radio, and print.[11] In 2016, 25 percent of evening broadcast journalists, 38 percent of print journalists, and 46 percent of internet journalists were women.[12] We're seeing more women in key roles as TV anchors and journalists, and just like their audience, they enjoy interviewing women because they relate to them better.

WOMEN ARE GOOD AT BUILDING RELATIONSHIPS

Publicity is very much about building relationships with the media. Studies on leadership traits have shown that women outshine men when it comes to building relationships. Of course, anyone can have a great PR campaign if they're willing to put in the time and effort it takes to build those relationships with the media. But for women, the efforts involved with a great publicity campaign may come more naturally.

❖ ❖ ❖

---

11 Linda Steiner, "Gender and Journalism," *Oxford Research Encyclopedia of Communication*, February 27, 2017, https://doi.org/10.1093/acrefore/9780190228613.013.91.

12 "Distribution of Journalists in the U.S. by Gender and Format 2016," Statista, accessed November 18, 2018, https://www.statista.com/statistics/625775/gender-news-reporitng-us.

The media tend to see women as the ones who can speak directly to the concerns and interests of that highly coveted female audience—and it's not a misconception. Women relate better to other women. Women talk differently than men. Women do business differently than men. Women handle their affairs differently. And women are more aware of what's happening in society relative to women in general, and how issues affect them.

The women's movement has come a long way, and as more and more women step out as professionals and have a voice, we will continue to make a difference. To my fellow women entrepreneurs: you can be a part of that difference and change the world for generations of women to come by following your career of choice and living your dream to its fullest.

To the men reading this book, don't despair! None of this means you can't also have a successful PR campaign. Instead, my hope is that you empower yourself with this information about trends in the media, and the impact of women as the biggest consumers, and use it to your advantage in your marketing and PR efforts.

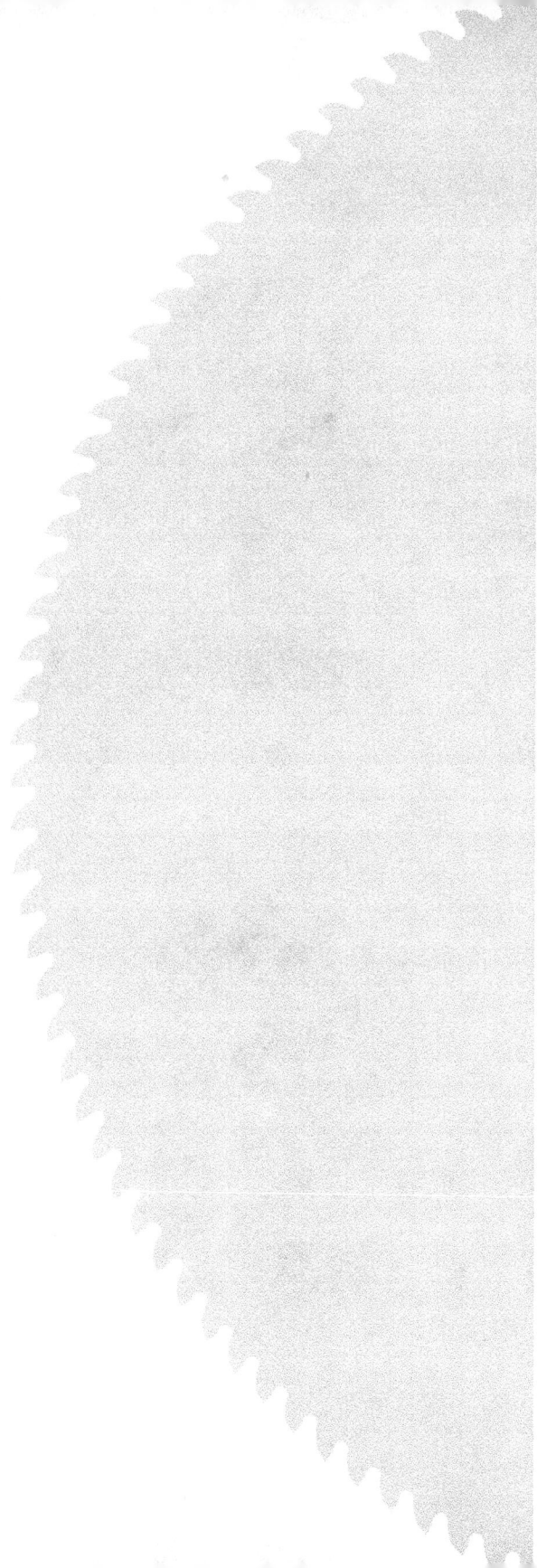

CHAPTER NINE

DON'T WANT TO GO IT ALONE? HOW TO HIRE THE BEST PR FIRM FOR YOU

f you plan to pursue media yourself, it takes a commitment of
time to start gaining the media's recognition. If you're too busy
running your business, then it's best to hire a good agency to do the
work for you. Then you get to be the talent, needed only for those
media interviews, rather than doing all the behind-scenes legwork of
arranging them.

Hiring a PR firm can be a confusing and daunting task. PR
companies differ in a multitude of ways. They use different business
models. They charge for services differently. They also have a whole
range of specialties, from crisis communications to public affairs to
research and analysis. How can you determine which is the right firm
for you and your needs?

FIND A FIRM THAT HAS A GOOD TRACK RECORD WITH CLIENTS IN YOUR INDUSTRY

The public relations industry has specialists in almost every field. A
firm that specializes in your industry understands that industry's par-
ticularities, its special terms, what's significant, what's newsworthy,
and what's not. That firm will likely have strong media relationships
with journalists and publications of interest to you. A good firm will
know where their expertise lies.

HIRE A FIRM THAT SPECIALIZES IN THE RIGHT MEDIA FOR YOU

Most PR firms specialize in print media (getting editorial coverage in
newspapers and magazines), and a growing number are focusing on
social media. But your audience may be watching TV talk shows, or
you may like the convenience and immediacy of talk radio. The firm
should be able to help you determine whether a particular medium

is appropriate for your message and audience, and it should have a strong track record in gaining clients exposure in that medium.

Some PR firms specialize only in local media. Don't choose a local firm when you need regional or national media exposure. After the initial meeting, your PR firm will require little face time with you, so don't concern yourself about where the firm is located. Just look for the best firm, period. Our firm, for example, is in the Tampa Bay area of Florida, but we have clients nationwide and even in other countries.

GET SAMPLES …

Ask to see samples of campaigns for clients. Yes, the agency will put its best foot forward, but the sample campaign they present to you demonstrates their skill and proficiency at obtaining media exposure. Keep in mind that a number of variables influence the success of a campaign and they're not all within the agency's control. Still, this should give you a good idea of their track record.

I frequently send samples to prospective clients. I have approval from some of my clients to share their campaign summaries and reports, so the prospect can see an actual example of what to expect. You want to have an idea of not only the quantity of media, but also the quality of the media relationships the agency works with.

… AND REFERENCES!

Additionally, get names of other clients they've represented and contact them to ask about the firm's weaknesses and strengths. Find out how quickly their account manager responded to their needs. How collaborative are they? How creative are they? Will that collaboration and creativity last? I have a new client who left their old agency because, after a year, the client was the one coming up with all the ideas, creating all the stories, and writing all the articles. You want to be sure the firm will continue working with you and for you, no matter how long your contract lasts. Ask the other clients if they would hire the firm again. And, most importantly, ask what results they got.

I would also encourage you to ask who is going to be working on your campaign. In a lot of big agencies, the partners of the firm are the rainmakers bringing in clients, which they then turn over to a less experienced associate to run the actual campaign. If you're paying big money to work with the best, that's who you want to work with. So find out who will be managing your account, and speak with their previous clients to find out what the experience was like.

UNDERSTAND THE FEE STRUCTURE

Make sure you understand the fee structure. For example, many retainer firms add charges for actions they take on your behalf, so in addition to the monthly retainer, you may be billed for materials they write for the press, time spent on research, phone charges, copying, and so on. This can make it hard to plan your budget.

One of the reasons I chose to use a "pay-for-performance" model in my company was to ensure that clients would leave satisfied. I prefer this approach over the retainer-fee model, which can cost a client thousands of dollars a month with no guarantee of results.

Whatever fee model the agency uses, make sure you understand it so you can have an accurate sense of what it will cost.

FIND THE FIRM THAT FEELS RIGHT

The most important thing is to find a company that understands you, your business, and your industry and, most importantly, that is as enthusiastic about your message as you are. PR firms are in the business of promotion; to succeed, they must be interested in what you're promoting. I frequently turn away business if the topic isn't a right fit, because I know we wouldn't do the best job. It's only fair to the prospective client. The firm pitching them to the media must thoroughly believe in what they do—and that's what I tell every prospect I reject.

Hire a firm that you feel comfortable with and would enjoy working with. If all the other criteria match, you should have no problem with this last one. If the PR firm that you hire truly supports your cause and is a real member of your "team," it can be a very rewarding experience. I've built many long-term relationships and associations with clients that go far beyond promoting their company, product, book, or service.

❖ ❖ ❖

Should We Continue the Conversation?

At News & Experts, we understand the importance of a perfect match between entrepreneur and PR firm. If, after reading this book, you are considering hiring a PR firm and are wondering if News & Experts might be the right fit, I'd love to share a little more about who we are and what we do.

News & Experts serves entrepreneurs, professionals, and CEOs who understand the power of publicity to build their personal and corporate brands.

Our specialty is media relationships, and we focus on all four types of media: press, radio, television, and social media. As you have learned, each of the media venues are different and requires different pitches and approaches. That's why, rather than having one account manager who deals with all media, as is typical in most agencies, our campaign managers are specialists in the media they work with.

If you think News & Experts might be the right PR firm for you, we'd love to continue the conversation. We enjoy speaking with prospective clients because we want to discover everything about you and your business to make sure you are a fit for our service and that we can deliver the goals you're looking to accomplish with your PR campaign.

❊ ❊ ❊

It may seem far-fetched to think that you could be quoted in *The New York Times* or *The Wall Street Journal* or that you could be on national television or talk radio shows. But I'm here to tell you—it can happen. And it can happen a lot sooner than you think. It's what we do every day for our clients.

I didn't build my agency working with people who were already celebrities. Instead, I wanted to work with people who have a desire to make a difference by sharing their valuable expertise. If your goal is to become a thought leader in your industry and make a difference in our society and the world, I hope I have given you some tools to help you achieve that goal.

There's no better time than now to get started. I'm looking forward to seeing you spotlighted in the media as you gain the publicity edge and change the world!

APPENDIX

MEDIA PITCH FORMATS

RADIO AND TELEVISION PITCHES

Radio and television pitches are very similar, and you can follow the same format for each, with one exception. For TV, you will want to include a description of the visual elements you can provide for the segment.

HEADLINE

Think of the headline as what the host or anchors will use to "tease" the segment to get viewers or listeners to stay tuned in. Often this is positioned as a question but can also be an attention-grabbing statement that will spark the interest of the audience.

TEASER

The first paragraph of the pitch should also act as a teaser—but in this case, teasing the producer to want to read more (i.e., recent news, statistics, and so on). This paragraph should be no longer than

143

two or three sentences, bolding any major news source or important information.

INTRODUCTION

The second paragraph introduces you, stating your name and most credible title that is relevant to the segment topic. This is usually followed by your book title if you are an author or some additional credentials about why you are able to speak on the topic. Make sure to BOLD your name and title.

TOPIC OVERVIEW

The third paragraph typically addresses the problem the audience has and the solution you will provide.

TALKING POINTS

Provide five or six questions the host can ask you. These questions should reflect exactly what you want the listeners to get out of the interview. The questions should be listed in an order that will bring you through the interview, enabling you to get your message out.

On your TV pitch, after the talking points, add the description of your visual elements.

CREDENTIALS

This section should begin with the most relevant information about you that follows the angle of the pitch. Any important information about you, including published works, awards, degrees, and so on should be listed here. Remember, only details relevant to your expert status on the show pitch should be included, and all unnecessary details should be omitted. This section should end with your Web address.

The last sentence of the pitch should state any prior TV appearances (especially national shows) and/or any experience on well-known radio shows or in print publications.

CONTACT INFORMATION

The pitch closes by asking if they'd like to schedule an interview. Make sure to include a phone number and/or email address where you can be reached.

AP-STYLE ARTICLES FOR PRINT

Generally, the AP-style articles we write are tips articles—now commonly known as "listicles." This is a great format, because it clearly and simply offers up the problem or issue and your advice or solutions. Here's the standard format we follow:

HEADLINE AND SUBHEAD

The headline, like those of radio and TV pitches, should be short and eye-catching. If it does not introduce the article as one that is tips oriented, then a subhead needs to be added that introduces the tips aspect. For example:

(Headline) Are You Waking Up Happy?

(Subhead) 5 Tips to Beat Depression

TOPIC INTRODUCTION

The first paragraph introduces the problem/topic that the tips will address. Build the case with relevant stats (if necessary) and other pieces of compelling information, which will grab the reader's interest.

EXPERT INTRODUCTION

The second or third paragraph introduces you (and mentions your website) as an expert on the topic. You could be an expert through your experience, your studies, your profession, to name a few possibilities, but this is not a review of your product or service, nor is it a sales pitch. Add a blatant sales pitch ("Read more about this in my book!" or "Contact my office to make an appointment with me today!") and you risk eliminating the chance of getting any coverage at all. Instead, focus on how you as an expert can help the readers by providing valuable information.

TIPS SECTION

After this is established, use the third paragraph as a transition into the tips portion of the article. The tips section should contain three to five tips. Here's where formatting is especially important: each tip should be bulleted or numbered.

The introduction of the tip should communicate EXACTLY what the tip is and should be bolded. The next few sentences should explain it a bit more. The final step for each is to give a clear example of how the tip can be applied.

For example, here's what that might look like if the tips were about beating depression:

1. Block Out Negative Influences. To beat depression, identify who around you—friends AND family—are having a negative impact on you. Surround yourself with those who are supportive and give encouragement. Join a local book club or society that shares in your interests.

Repeat this for each of the tips.

SUMMARY

After all of the tips have been stated and defined, and applicable examples have been provided, the article should have a final paragraph that brings it all together.

VISUALS

You can offer to provide good quality photographs to support your story if photographs are appropriate to the article.

DON'T FORGET TO PROOFREAD!

Remember that in all cases the content must be professional. Publications don't accept just anything that comes across their email. They look for professional work, free of typos, grammatical errors, and spelling mistakes. Editors don't have the time or patience to read pointless ramblings or endure the headache of editing an article littered with errors. The goal is to make their work easier, not harder!

ABOUT THE AUTHOR

Marsha Friedman, a leader and innovator in the field of public relations, is a true believer in the power of publicity and has dedicated her career to raising the bar and educating her followers. For nearly thirty years, she has developed publicity strategies for celebrities, corporations, CEOs, and professionals in a broad range of industries. She is the founder and president of News & Experts, an award-winning national public relations agency that secures thousands of top-tier media placements annually for their clients. Her firm is a trusted provider of news and feature articles, as well as a resource for journalists and producers seeking qualified experts to address topical news, issues and trends. With the goal of building a bigger brand that impacts more people, News & Experts formally joined the Advantage family in 2018.

Marsha's first book, *Celebritize Yourself: The Three Step Method to Increasing Your Profile and Exploding Your Business* is an Amazon bestseller. She speaks at conferences and events across the country. Her entertaining and insightful anecdotes, her unique teaching approach on harnessing the power of publicity, and her uncanny ability to connect with audiences from a variety of diverse industries have positioned Marsha among the elite.

When she's not helping people with their publicity efforts, Marsha is busy as wife to her husband, Steve, and enjoys spending time with their four children and grandchildren.

After twenty-nine years in the industry, you might think that Marsha Friedman would be ready to relax and slow down, but you would be sorely mistaken. She's moving full speed ahead and relishing every minute of the ride.

OUR SERVICES

Pick up a newspaper, turn on the TV or radio, or log onto a news website and you will discover a plethora of experts offering insights on the day's events or providing tips to help readers, viewers, or listeners improve their lives. But these experts and the media didn't find each other by happenstance—as you are about to learn.

Gaining the Publicity Edge reveals how to build your brand by becoming one of the go-to people the media turn to again and again. For nearly three decades, author Marsha Friedman has been at the helm of one of the most successful boutique PR firms in the US, helping thousands of top professionals develop and enjoy the status of being known in the media and in society at large as leading authorities in their fields. Now she will share with you her knowledge of how to get the attention of the national media and become a voice of authority they rely on—while in the process, gaining an edge over your competition. You will learn how to

- understand the needs of the media;

- successfully pitch yourself to journalists, producers, and hosts;

- determine which medium is the best match for you and your message;

- give a great interview; and

- leverage your media coverage to build your brand as an expert.

Once you grasp how the media work and what they need, you'll be on your way to growing your brand through the coverage you deserve as an expert in your field!

VISIT US ONLINE TO ACCESS THESE FREE RESOURCES

How do your press hits rank against your competitors?

When the media needs a reliable source to interview for their publication or on their show, they look to a select few experts to answer the call. Do you qualify to be one of their go-to authorities?

→ **Take the assessment at newsandexperts.com/assessment to find out.**
Your score will be emailed to you within seconds of submitting.

Subscribe to our newsletter.

Sign up for the PR Insider Newsletter to receive weekly publicity tips to get you featured in the press and on radio and TV.

→ **Subscribe at newsandexperts.com/newsletter.**

Get In Touch

Our team is always ready to assist you with all your Public Relations needs and we look forward to your questions and comments.

→ **Reach out by emailing info@newsandexperts.com or calling 800.204.7115.**

A Special Offer
from
ForbesBooks

www.ingramcontent.com/pod-product-compliance
Lightning Source LLC
Chambersburg PA
CBHW050528190326
41458CB00045B/6750/J